ATTACKING HEZBOLLAH'S FINANCIAL NETWORK: POLICY OPTIONS

HEARING

BEFORE THE

COMMITTEE ON FOREIGN AFFAIRS
HOUSE OF REPRESENTATIVES

ONE HUNDRED FIFTEENTH CONGRESS

FIRST SESSION

JUNE 8, 2017

Serial No. 115–51

Printed for the use of the Committee on Foreign Affairs

Available via the World Wide Web: http://www.foreignaffairs.house.gov/ or
http://www.gpo.gov/fdsys/

U.S. GOVERNMENT PUBLISHING OFFICE

25–730PDF   WASHINGTON : 2017

CONTENTS

Page

ATTACKING HEZBOLLAH'S FINANCIAL NETWORK: POLICY OPTIONS

THURSDAY, JUNE 8, 2017

House of Representatives,
Committee on Foreign Affairs,
Washington, DC.

The committee met, pursuant to notice, at 10:08 a.m., in room 2172, Rayburn House Office Building, Hon. Edward Royce (chairman of the committee) presiding.

Chairman ROYCE. This hearing will come to order. This hearing is on attacking Hezbollah's financial network, and different policy options that we have. So we consider these additional steps needed to confront one of the top terror threats in the world, and that threat is Hezbollah. It is a terrorist group that is based in Lebanon, where it is a significant political force as well. If you look at the history, it dates back to 1982 when members of Tehran's Revolutionary Guard Corps' Quds Force first deployed in Lebanon's Beqaa Valley. And they created, armed, and funded a small force which became Hezbollah.

Today, as the leading Iranian proxy, Hezbollah continues to be Iran's front line against Israel. Since its 2006 war with Israel, Hezbollah has dramatically grown its supply of rockets and missiles, allowing it to strike throughout Israel, with much greater precision and force.

I was in Haifa in 2006, and at that point in time, there were 10,000 of these rockets fired out of an inventory of about 20,000. I saw the consequence of it. There were 600 victims from Haifa in the trauma hospital who were being treated as a result of the attacks on civilian neighborhoods.

It is 11 years since that period of time, and now, instead of 10,000 rockets and missiles remaining in the inventory, there are 110,000, and these are of increasing sophistication. One observer even wrote that Hezbollah is now, in his words, "more militarily powerful than most North Atlantic treaty organization members." One of reasons for this, by the way, is that many of these newer missiles Iran is working on developing—and I am talking about the government, Iran's Islamic Revolutionary Guard Corps—is working on the ability to make these GPS-guided missiles.

Hezbollah is putting its military power to very effective use. In Syria, its fighters are key to the efforts by Iran's Islamic Revolutionary Guard Corps and Moscow's efforts to prop up the Assad regime, along with Russian troops and Iran's Revolutionary Guards.

For 30 years, Hezbollah has remained Iran's proxy, and Iran remains Hezbollah's primary source of financial support. In April 2015, its leader, Hassan Nasrallah, boasted that even under sanctions, Iran still funded Hezbollah's terror war. And he anticipated that a rich—in his words, "a rich and powerful Iran, which will be open to the world," would be able to do even more. The Iran nuclear agreement has made it possible for Iran to provide Hezbollah with a windfall. As one witness will testify today, Hezbollah's activities since the nuclear agreement have "expanded in scope."

But Tehran is not Hezbollah's only source of income, because since its inception, Hezbollah has developed a broad criminal network involved in a range of illegal activities—from drug trafficking, to cigarette smuggling, to money laundering, to counterfeiting. These global terrorists double as global criminals.

Indeed, in February 2016, the U.S. Drug Enforcement Administration—in an operation led by one of the witnesses who is here with us today—implicated Hezbollah in a multimillion dollar drug traffic and money laundering network that spanned four continents and put cocaine ultimately on the streets of the United States.

The committee is focused on the best way to attack Hezbollah's financial network and its tentacles across the globe. And in 2015, we led the way to enact the Hezbollah International Financing Prevention Act to target those that facilitate financial transactions for Hezbollah. This has helped put Hezbollah in the "worst financial shape in decades," according to the top Treasury official, despite Iran's continued support. Part two of this legislation is coming, but, unfortunately, that is of little comfort to Israelis staring down at an arsenal of rockets that sit just across the border from Lebanon or the Syrians being slaughtered at the hands of Hezbollah operatives that are participating in ethnic cleansing in Syria.

We look forward to hearing from our witnesses today on ways in which the United States can further tighten the grip.

I now yield to our ranking member today, Mr. Deutch, for any opening comments he may have.

Mr. DEUTCH. Thank you, Mr. Chairman. I would like to thank you and Mr. Engel for holding today's hearing on what is arguably one of the greatest threats to U.S. security interests and the interests of so many of our allies. And thanks to the witnesses for being here today as well.

Hezbollah is a terrorist organization that has attempted to carry out, or has successfully carried out, attacks on multiple continents, from the bombing on in the U.S. Marine barracks in 1983, to the bombing of a Jewish center in Argentina in 1994, to the bus bombings in Bulgaria in 2012. Hezbollah's reign of terror has no geographical boundaries.

Perhaps most concerning in recent years has been Hezbollah's entry into Syria. Working on behalf of the murderous Assad regime, there are estimated to be 7,000 Hezbollah fighters inside Syria. Receiving significant military support from Iran, Hezbollah, along with various Iranian-backed militias, has assisted the Assad regime in devastating attacks on the Syrian people.

In turn, ISIS-affiliated retaliatory attacks have been launched inside Lebanon, killing innocent Lebanese civilians. Hezbollah's involvement in Syria has fed the emergence of the Russia-Iran-Assad alliance. Open source reporting now details the transfer of advanced weaponry from Russia to Hezbollah. It is reported that Hezbollah is in possession of Russian designed surface-to-air shoulder-mounted missiles. This is in addition to the precision-guided missiles it is apparently now receiving from Iran that will add to its arsenal of over 120,000 rockets capable of reaching every corner of Israel. And Hezbollah is now sending fighters to Iraq and to Yemen.

Let me be clear: There can be no future in Syria where Iran and/or Hezbollah has a permanent, military presence. And it remains to be seen how this administration thinks that it can cooperate with Russia and Syria when Russia has so far been unwilling to separate itself from Iranian efforts to strengthen Assad.

Last month, Hezbollah's leader, Hassan Nasrallah, stated that the conflict had entered what he described as a new and critical phase in which Damascus, Moscow, Tehran, and Hezbollah were, and I quote, "in more harmony politically and militarily than at any time."

Hezbollah has long received hundreds of millions of dollars a year from Iran. However, Hezbollah has expended its own financing operations to include what has become known as the business affairs component, a transnational criminal network that engages in everything from narcotrafficking to money laundering, to the sale of counterfeit cigarettes and goods. These operations have gained significant foothold in Latin America, in Europe, and in Africa. Increased cooperation between U.S. law enforcement and law enforcement entities around the world has resulted in significant exposure and breakup of many of Hezbollah's illicit financing networks. Project Cassandra, a DEA-led effort, which we will hear more about from our witnesses, exposed a massive narcotrafficking ring.

International cooperation is crucial to our efforts to disrupt Hezbollah. And this is precisely why our allies in Europe must join the United States, the GCC, Canada and others in designating the whole of Hezbollah as a terrorist organization. The idea that there is separation between Hezbollah's military and political wings is, quite frankly, laughable, which is why I recently introduced a resolution urging that you designate Hezbollah, in its entirety, as a terrorist organization.

I am proud to be joined by a bipartisan group of members in this effort, including members of this committee, our chairman emeritus Ros-Lehtinen, and Mr. Lieu, Mr. Zeldin, and Mr. Schneider.

Congress has played a significant role in preventing funds from flowing to Hezbollah. In 2015, I was proud to join Chairman Royce in introducing and passing the Hezbollah International Financing Prevention Act. And I just want to note that when we first introduced those new sanctions, we were told, as we so often are warned against the perils of using economic sanctions, that the Lebanese banking sector would collapse. But through the work of this committee and outreach to those Lebanese banks, that has not been the case. In fact, Lebanon's central bank has shut down the accounts of Hezbollah members and affiliates. But there is more that we can do. Secondary sanctions, for one, proved extremely effective in our policy toward Iran.

Today provides us with an opportunity to hear from our witnesses new policy prescriptions for cracking down on Hezbollah, both on the military and terrorism fronts, and ways to stop its funding streams.

Mr. Chairman, before turning back over, I would ask unanimous consent to enter into the record a statement by the Anti-Defamation League supporting new legislative efforts to crack down on Hezbollah's funding.

Chairman ROYCE. Without objection.

Mr. DEUTCH. I appreciate that. I look forward to this committee working together, as we regularly do, in a bipartisan manner under your leadership, Mr. Chairman, to move forward with these new efforts. I thank you and I yield back.

Mr. CONNOLLY. Mr. Chairman, if I could just add, I have joined in the resolution so there are other members as well.

Mr. DEUTCH. I thank my friend from Virginia.

Chairman ROYCE. Thank you, Mr. Connolly.

This morning, we are pleased to be joined be a very distinguished panel. We have Dr. Matt Levitt, a director at the Washington Institute for Near East Policy. And he previously served as a senior official at the Treasury Department. He has written extensively on Hezbollah.

We also have Dr. David Asher. He is a member of the board at the Foundation for Defense of Democracies, and he has played a senior role in numerous economic and financial pressure campaigns. He was an early pioneer in tackling North Korea's proliferation network.

We also have Mr. Derek Maltz with us, the executive director of government relations at Pen-Link. Previously, Mr. Maltz led the Drug Enforcement Administration's special operations division in actively targeting narcotics trafficking tied to Hezbollah.

We have Dr. Mara Karlin, associate professor with the Johns Hopkins School of Advanced International Studies. She previously served as an aide to the Under Secretary for Policy at the Department of Defense with a focus on the Levant.

So without objection, the witnesses' full prepared statements will be made a part of the record, and members will have 5 calendar days to submit any statements or questions or extraneous material for the record. We will start with Dr. Levitt, and we will ask you to summarize your remarks.

STATEMENT OF MATTHEW LEVITT, PH.D., DIRECTOR AND FROMER-WEXLER FELLOW, STEIN PROGRAM ON COUNTER-TERRORISM AND INTELLIGENCE, THE WASHINGTON INSTITUTE FOR NEAR EAST POLICY

Mr. LEVITT. Thank you, Chairman, Mr. Deutch, members of the committee. It is a pleasure to be here to testify before you today, and assess our efforts and those pursued to date to counter Hezbollah's ability to exploit the international financial system to its benefit. The regional international threats posed by Hezbollah have only increased over time, underscoring the importance of denying the group the financing and resources critical to its ability to function.

Hezbollah has, in fact, experienced a series of financial setbacks, in part because of the actions we have taken, leading U.S. officials to describe the group as being "in the worst financial shape in decades." In recent months, Hezbollah has resorted to launching an online fundraising, crowd-sourcing campaign entitled Equip a Mujahid Campaign, which calls for donations large and small, payable all at once, or in installments, to equip Hezbollah fighters. It has also promoted a fundraising campaign on billboards and posters in Lebanon, promoting a program in which supporters can avoid recruitment into Hezbollah's militia forces for a payment of about $1,000. These are desperate measures for a group suffering through tough financial times. And yet it has enough money to do a great many disturbing things around the world.

I should stress here that of the various actions we are suggesting, that I am suggesting and others, the idea is not to undermine the Lebanese economy, but to protect it from exposure to the criminal and money-laundering enterprises in which Hezbollah is deeply involved. It should, therefore, not surprise that after Congress passed the Hezbollah International Finance Prevention Act, Lebanon Central Bank issued a circular ordering Lebanese banks to close accounts belonging to individuals and institutions associated with Hezbollah. According to the Central Bank, hundreds of Hezbollah-linked accounts have since been closed.

Now Hezbollah continues to operate in Europe, despite the partial ban in July 2013, and it is aggressively engaged in criminal enterprises and Africa and in South America. And despite being designated as a terrorist group by the Gulf Cooperation Council, Hezbollah reportedly began storing some of its funds outside Lebanon in response to the effects of the HIFPA legislation, including in places like Iraq and Dubai.

Now, Hezbollah continues to get significant support from Iran, but I think today I want to focus on its global criminal enterprise. Now I am going to leave the business affairs components and other things to my colleagues. What I want to highlight here are some of other successes. For example, the extent of Hezbollah's drug connection was underscored in the wake of the U.S. Treasury's narcotics kingpin designation of the Panama based Waked Money Laundering Organization in May 2016. This action wasn't taken under a terrorism authority, and the press release said nothing about Hezbollah, but when this particular money laundering organization was targeted, it tied up the illicit finances linked to various elements within the Iran threat network, including Hezbollah, and forced them to find other money laundering channels in the region. Much of that activity reportedly shifted to the Tri-Border Area, and to Paraguay in particular. Hezbollah criminal enterprises run deep in Africa, as evidenced most recently by the arrest in Morocco, Hezbollah financier Kassim Tajideen, who has since been extradited to the United States and indicted in Washington, DC.

There a bunch of steps I think we can do to further actions we have already taken. The first is to designate additional Hezbollah entities as appropriate. HIFPA prescribes doing business with designated Hezbollah entities. So the more a Hezbollah entity is designated, the more impactful the legislation will be. This should include, but not be limited to, entities operating in Lebanon. For example, consider the list of Lebanese businesses designated with Lebanon-based IRGC Quds Force operative, Hasan Ebrahimi, in February.

Targeting Hezbollah criminal enterprises in South America, Africa, and Europe will be very important as well. Again, think about the Waked money laundering organization and that success. And finally, in this regard, consider follow-on actions to existing designations where appropriate. For example, the IRGC official in Lebanon, Ebrahimi, was providing Hezbollah funds through Hezbollah's al Waad construction firm, which we had already designated in 2009 or this Equip a Mujahid Campaign in Lebanon is being run by the Islamic Resistance Support Organization, IRSO, which Treasury already designated back in 2006.

Second, we should target Hezbollah criminal support networks of a variety of different types. I get into those in my testimony.

Third, we should consider applying secondary sanctions under HIFPA to financial institutions banking Hezbollah, its associates outside the Middle East. And here, for example, I think we should look at places like Balboa Bank & Trust, which was designated by Treasury in the context of the action taken against the Waked money laundering organization.

We should revisit the question of designating Hezbollah a transnational criminal organization, which it absolutely is without question. We should resume sanctioning Iran for state sponsorship of terrorism.

Again, we saw the Ebrahimi action in February, but the Quds Force, Mahan Air—a whole host of other low-hanging fruit, Iranian entities involved in Tehran's support for terrorism—should be designated. And this, in no way, would jeopardize or conflict with the JCPOA Iran deal.

And finally, we absolutely must continue to enhance interagency coordination and cooperation against the Iran threat network. That began to fall apart a little bit in the context of the Iran deal where some agencies wanted to push harder and some did not. Today there is, I think, greater consensus on the need to push hard on the maligned activities that Iran is engaged in beyond procurement, such as support for terrorism. And I think that there is a lot more we can do here. There are positive signs, on this I will conclude, for example, of using the global counterterrorism forum, the law enforcement and coordination group, both to address best practices for countering Hezbollah terrorist, criminal, and other terrorist activities that have been a great success. The State Department, similarly, has used the counterterrorism partnership fund to launch an international initiative in very close partnership with the Department of Justice to raise awareness about Iran and Hezbollah's broad range of terrorist and criminal activities around the world, and to help train our allies around the world to figure out how best to prosecute and deal with those activities. These types of efforts should be doubled down on. There is a lot more we can do. I thank you for the opportunity to testify before you today.

[The prepared statement of Mr. Levitt follows:]

Attacking Hezbollah's Financial Network: Policy Options

Dr. Matthew Levitt

Fromer-Wexler Fellow and Director, Stein Program on Counterterrorism and Intelligence,
The Washington Institute for Near East Policy

Testimony submitted to the Committee on Foreign Affairs, U.S. House of Representatives

June 8, 2017

Chairman Royce, Ranking Member Engel, and Members of the Committee, thank you for this opportunity to appear before you today to assess efforts pursued to date to counter Hezbollah's ability to exploit the international financial system to its benefit, and to propose policy options to more effectively target Hezbollah's bottom line.

The regional and international threats posed by Hezbollah have only increased over time, underscoring the importance of denying the group the financing and resources that are critical to its ability to function. Hezbollah has experienced a series of financial setbacks, leading U.S. officials to describe the group being in the "worst financial shape in decades."[1] Indeed, Hezbollah has in recent months resorted to launching an online fundraising crowdsourcing campaign entitled "Equip a Mujahid Campaign" which calls for donations, large or small, payable all at once or in instalments, to equip Hezbollah fighters.[2] Hezbollah has also promoted a fundraising campaign on billboards and posters promoting a program through which supporters whereby supporters can avoid recruitment into Hezbollah's militia forces for a payment of about $1,000.[3] These are desperate measures for a group suffering tough financial times.

And yet, Hezbollah continues to collect sufficient funds to deploy a significant militia at home and next door in Syria, to send smaller groups of operatives to Iraq and Yemen, and to operate an international terrorist network with deadly effect. To effectively counter Hezbollah's financing, the U.S. must lead an international effort to target the group's illicit financial conduct both at home in Lebanon and around the world. The idea here is not to undermine the Lebanese economy, but to protect it from exposure to the criminal and money laundering enterprises in

---

[1] "Hezbollah in 'worst financial shape in decades,' US says," The Times of Israel, May 25, 2016, http://www.timesofisrael.com/hezbollah-in-worst-financial-shape-in-decades-us-says/
[2] "Hizbullah Launches Online Fundraising Campaign," MEMRI, February 10, 2017, http://cjlab.memri.org/lab-projects/tracking-jihadi-terrorist-use-of-social-media/hizbullah-launches-online-fundraising-campaign/
[3] "Hezbollah Asks for Support on Billboards and Posters," Al Arabiya, June 7, 2017, https://english.alarabiya.net/en/News/middle-east/2017/06/07/Hezbollah-asks-for-support-on-billboards.html

which Hezbollah is deeply involved. It should therefore not surprise that after Congress passed the Hezbollah International Finance Prevention Act (HIFPA), Lebanon's central bank issued a circular ordering Lebanese banks to close accounts belonging to individuals and institutions associated with Hezbollah. According to the central bank, hundreds of Hezbollah-linked accounts have since been closed.

Similarly, outreach to foreign partners regarding Hezbollah is based not only on the increasingly shared position that Hezbollah is an international terrorist group, but also on the universal position that the group is deeply involved in criminal enterprises that put national economies and the international financial system at risk. Hezbollah continues to operate in Europe even after the ban placed on parts of the group (it's military and terrorist wings) in July 2013, and is aggressively engaged in criminal enterprises in Africa and South America. Despite being designated a terrorist group by the Gulf Cooperation Council (GCC), Hezbollah reportedly began storing some of its funds outside Lebanon in response to the effect of the HIFPA legislation, including in places like Iraq and Dubai.

Hezbollah's Transformation

The war in Syria has dramatically changed Hezbollah. Once limited to jockeying for political power in Lebanon and fighting Israel, the group is now a regional player engaged in conflicts far beyond its historical area of operations (Iraq and Yemen), often in cooperation with Iran. The strongest indicators of Hezbollah's transformation are structural. Since 2013, the group has added two new commands—the first on the Lebanese–Syrian border, the second within Syria itself—to its existing bases in southern and eastern Lebanon. In establishing its new presence in Syria, Hezbollah has also transferred key personnel from its traditionally paramount Southern Command, along Lebanon's border with Israel.

In addition to the traditional Lebanese Hezbollah, which has been deploying fighters to Syria since 2011, Islamic Revolutionary Guard Corps (IRGC) General Hossein Hamedani declared in May 2014 that Iran had formed "a second Hezbollah in Syria." In early 2014, several Shiite militias in Syria began to call themselves, "Hezbollah fi Suriya," or Hezbollah in Syria. Inspired by the success of Lebanese Hezbollah, Iran had begun to build a Syrian wing of the movement, to "carry out ideological as well as other regional power-projection goals."[4] While most of their actions so far have been limited to Syria, Hezbollah fi Suriya has made calls to unify with other Shia militia groups in Iraq as well. The Hezbollization of these groups, in name, structure, and allegiance, signifies a major accomplishment for Tehran, allowing Iran to preserve harder-core influence and more effectively project power within and beyond Syria.[5]

Iranian support for Hezbollah is believed to continue at the same level it has been at for several years, but more of that money now goes to underwrite Hezbollah activities in Syria than in Lebanon. That is putting significant pressure on Hezbollah back home in Lebanon, where tensions are rising over the group's lack of support for its constituent base.[6] This, in turn, has led

---

[4] Philip Smyth, "How Iran Is Building Its Syrian Hezbollah," *The Washington Institute for Near East Policy,* March 8, 2016, https://www.washingtoninstitute.org/policy-analysis/view/how-iran-is-building-its-syrian-hezbollah

[5] Philip Smyth, "How Iran Is Building Its Syrian Hezbollah." *The Washington Institute for Near East Policy,* March 8, 2016, https://www.washingtoninstitute.org/policy-analysis/view/how-iran-is-building-its-syrian-hezbollah

[6] Hannin Ghadar. "Hezbollah's Women Aren't Happy'" *The Washington Institute*, October 12, 2016, http://www.washingtoninstitute.org/policy-analysis/view/hezbollahs-women-arent-happy

to an ideological crisis for the group because many of its fighters no longer see the war in Syria as a sacred battle.[7]

Even as it deepens its activities in Syria, Hezbollah continues to aid Shiite militias in Iraq, sending small numbers of skilled trainers to train Shia militias and help defend Shiite shrines there. Indeed, Hassan Nasrallah admitted on March 6, 2016 that Hezbollah had covertly dispatched Hezbollah operatives to Iraq, "In Iraq, we fought under the Iraqi command and we did not interfere in their affairs. It is an ethical, humanitarian and pan-Arab duty," and he continued to say that some Hezbollah fighters remained in Iraq now because the Islamic State is still there. [8]

According to the U.S. Department of the Treasury, Hezbollah has also invested in commercial front organizations to support its operations in Iraq.[9] Hezbollah member Adham Tabaja, the majority owner of the Lebanon-based real estate and construction firm Al-Inmaa Group for Tourism Works, has exploited the firm's Iraqi subsidiaries to fund Hezbollah, with the assistance of Kassem Hejeij, a Lebanese businessman tied to Hezbollah, and Husayn Ali Faour, a member of Hezbollah's overseas terrorism unit.

And while the number of fighters Hezbollah has sent to Yemen to assist the Houthis may be small, that is certainly not a reflection of the importance with which they view the civil war there. Take for instance Khalil Harb, a former special operations commander and a close adviser to Nasrallah, oversees Hezbollah's activities in Yemen—managing the transfer of funds to the organization within the country—and travels frequently to Tehran to coordinate Hezbollah activities with Iranian officials. Given his experience working with other terrorist organizations, his close relations with Iranian and Hezbollah leaders, and his expertise with special operations and training, appointing Harb to work in Yemen no doubt made a great deal of sense to Hezbollah.

Harb, however, is not the most senior operative dispatched to Yemen by Hezbollah. In the spring of 2015, Hezbollah sent Abu Ali Tabtabai, the senior commander formerly stationed in Syria, to upgrade the group's training program for Yemen's Houthi rebels, which reportedly involves schooling them in guerilla tactics. "Sending in Tabtabai [to Yemen] is a sign of a major Hezbollah investment and commitment," an Israeli official told me. "The key question is how long someone of Tabtabai's stature will stay."[10]

---

[7] Hanin Ghaddar, "Economic Alternatives Could Help Split Shiites From Hezbollah." *The Washington Institute*, October 18, 201.http://www.washingtoninstitute.org/policy-analysis/view/economic-alternatives-could-help-split-shiites-from-hezbollah
[8] "Nasrallah: Hezbollah sent fighters to Iraq." *DailyStar Lebanon*, March 7, 2016, https://www.dailystar.com.lb/News/Lebanon-News/2016/Mar-07/340892-nasrallah-hezbollah-sent-fighters-to-iraq.ashx
[9] "Treasury Sanctions Hizballah Front Companies and Facilitators in Lebanon And Iraq." US Department of Treasury, June 10, 2015, https://www.treasury.gov/press-center/press-releases/Pages/jl0069.aspx
[10] Matthew Levitt, "Waking Up the Neighbors," *Foreign Affairs*, July 28, 2015, https://www.foreignaffairs.com/articles/israel/2015-07-23/waking-neighbors

Beyond Iraq and Yemen, Hezbollah cells have been uncovered in Bahrain, Kuwait and the UAE as well.[11]

Global Criminal Enterprise

To further its operational objectives, Hezbollah relies on a worldwide network of supporters and sympathizers to provide financial, logistical, and operational support. These include both informal networks of supporters and centrally-run enterprises that effectively operate like international organized criminal organizations. The former provide small level financial or other support, as they are able. But the latter are relied upon for multi-million dollar funding schemes, for logistical support activities like setting up front and cover organizations, and to procure weapons, dual-use items, false documents, and more for the group. Of the former, few tend to be formal networks; often they are intentionally structured to be opaquely affiliated with Hezbollah as to avoid detection. But the latter, which also rely on relationships with criminal "super facilitators" who can move and launder massive amounts of money, for example, are involved in large-scale money laundering, drug smuggling, and arms sales.

Consider the arrests by the US Drug Enforcement Administration (DEA) and Europol that targeted what U.S. law enforcement now refer to as the Business Affairs Component (BAC) of Hezbollah's terrorist wing, the Islamic Jihad Organization (also known as the External Security Organization). Engaging in drug trafficking and drug smuggling, U.S. officials report that the BAC was founded by deceased Hezbollah Senior Leader Imad Mughniyah and currently operates under the control of senior Hezbollah official Abdallah Safieddine and recently designated Specially Designated Global Terrorist (SDGT) Adham Tabaja.[12]

The BAC established working relationships with South American drug cartels that supplied cocaine to drug markets in both the US and Europe. The BAC would then launder the drug proceeds through the well-known Black Market Peso Exchange. In late January 2016, the DEA and Customs and Border Protection coordinated with multiple foreign counterparts to arrest top leaders of Hezbollah's BAC, including U.S.-designated SDGT Mohamad Noureddine, who has worked directly with Hezbollah's financial apparatus to transfer Hezbollah funds via his Lebanon-based company Trade Point International S.A.R.L. and maintained direct ties to Hezbollah commercial and terrorist elements in both Lebanon and Iraq.[13] United States Department of Treasury similarly targeted Noureddine and his accomplice Hamdi Zaher El Dine and their company, Trade Point International S.A.R.L.[14]

Hezbollah's aggressive and ongoing procurement efforts have not been reigned in since the signing of the JCPOA, but have actually expanded in scope. These aggressive efforts span the

---

[11] Yara Bayoumy, "Kuwait court sentences two to death for spying for Iran, Hezbollah," Reuters, January 12, 2016, http://www.reuters.com/article/us-kuwait-security-idUSKCN0UQ0RS20160112; "Bahrain says it dismantled Iran-linked terror cell," Agence France-Presse, January 6, 2016, http://www.timesofisrael.com/bahrain-says-it-dismantled-iran-linked-terror-cell; Abdulla Rasheed, "Iran set up Hezbollah cell in UAE, court hears," Gulf News, April 18, 2016, http://gulfnews.com/news/uae/government/iran-set-up-hezbollah-cell-in-uae-court-hears-1.1715716

[12] "DEA and European Authorities Uncover Massive Hizballah Drug and Money Laundering Scheme," US Drug Enforcement Administration, February 1, 2016, http://www.dea.gov/divisions/hq/2016/hq020116.shtml

[13] "DEA and European Authorities Uncover Massive Hizballah Drug and Money Laundering Scheme," US Drug Enforcement Administration, February 1, 2016, http://www.dea.gov/divisions/hq/2016/hq020116.shtml

[14] "Treasury Sanctions Key Hizballah Money Laundering Network," US Department of Treasury, January 28, 2016, https://www.treasury.gov/press-center/press-releases/Pages/jl0331.aspx

globe, but have been especially pronounced in Europe and South America. Outside of the BAC arrests, United States Department of Treasury designated Hezbollah procurement agent Fadi Hussein Serhan, his company Vatech SARL, Hezbollah procurement agent Adel Mohamad Cherri and his company Le-Hua Electronics Field Co. Limited, and two companies owned or controlled by Specially Designated Global Terrorist and Hezbollah procurement agent Ali Zeaiter.[15]

Vatech SARL, run by Fadi Serhan, was designated for purchasing sensitive technology and equipment, including but not limited to UAVs on behalf of Hezbollah. Serhan sought these products from companies in the US, Europe, Asia and the Middle East. Adel Mohamad Cherri was attempting to procure a variety of electronics from China and send them to the Houthis in Yemen by using his company, Le-Hua Electronic Field Co. Ali Zeaiter's two companies, Aero Skyone Co. Limited and Labico SAL Offshore, were designated for again trying to procure UAV-related equipment through Europe and Asia.[16]

Investigation into Hezbollah BAC finance and facilitation networks has touched the United States as well. In October 2015, U.S. officials arrested Iman Kobeissi in Atlanta, Georgia. Kobeissi was arraigned on money laundering conspiracy charges and unlicensed firearms dealing conspiracy for laundering funds she believed to be drug money, and for arranging for the sale of thousands of firearms, including military assault rifles, machine guns, and sniper rifles, to criminal groups in Iran and Lebanon, including Hezbollah. The same day, her Hezbollah associate, Joseph Asmar, was arrested in Paris and charged with money laundering conspiracy.[17]

Hezbollah Operations in South America

The extent of Hezbollah's drug connection was underscored once more in the wake of the U.S. Treasury narcotics kingpin designation of the Panama-based Waked Money Laundering Organization in May 2016.[18] The press release tied to this action mentions neither Hezbollah nor Iran, but the action reportedly proved to be particularly damaging for both Hezbollah and Iranian illicit financial conduct in the region. When this particular money laundering organization was targeted, it tied up illicit finances linked to various Iran Threat Network entities, including Hezbollah, and forced them to find other money laundering channels in the region. Much of that activity reportedly shifted to the Tri-Border Area, and to Paraguay in particular.

The Tri-Border Area remains a place where Hezbollah and other militant and criminal organizations engage in a wide array of criminal activities, including the sale of stolen and

---

[15] "Treasury Sanctions Hizballah Procurement Agents and Their Companies," US Department of Treasury, November 5. 2015, https://www.treasury.gov/press-center/press-releases/Pages/jl0255.aspx
[16] "Treasury Sanctions Hizballah Procurement Agents and Their Companies," US Department of Treasury, November 5, 2015, https://www.treasury.gov/press-center/press-releases/Pages/jl0255.aspx

[17] "Two Hezbollah Associates Arrested On Charges Of Conspiring To Launder Narcotics Proceeds And International Arms Trafficking," US Attorney's Office Eastern District of New York, October 9, 2015, https://www.justice.gov/usao-edny/pr/two-hezbollah-associates-arrested-charges-conspiring-launder-narcotics-proceeds-and

[18] "Treasury Sanctions the Waked Money Laundering Organization," U.S. Department of the Treasury, May 5, 2016, https://www.treasury.gov/press-center/press-releases/Pages/jl0450.aspx

counterfeit goods. Indeed, Hezbollah profits from illegal tobacco trade around the world, including in Israel, according to a report issued by the Israeli Ministry of Health.[19]

Fifteen years ago this month, Hezbollah operative Assad Barakat was arrested in Brazil. Today, the Barakat clan reportedly remains active in the region[20] and Hezbollah activities in the region have picked up pace significantly. In its 2014 annual terrorism report the State Department highlighted the financial support networks Hezbollah maintains in places like Latin America and Africa. The report concluded that Hezbollah remains, "capable of operating around the globe."[21] This conclusion was underscored in November 2014 when Brazilian police reports revealed that Hezbollah helped a Brazilian prison gang, the First Capital Command (PCC), obtain weapons in exchange for the protection of prisoners of Lebanese origin detained in Brazil.[22] The same reports indicated that Lebanese traffickers tied to Hezbollah reportedly helped sell C4 explosives that the PCC allegedly stole in Paraguay.[23]

Peruvian counterterrorism police arrested a Hezbollah operative in Lima in November 2014, the result of a surveillance operation that began several months earlier. In that case, Mohammed Amadar, a Lebanese citizen, arrived in Peru in November 2013 and married a dual Peruvian-American citizen two weeks later. They soon moved to Brazil, living in Sao Paulo until they returned to Lima in July 2014. Authorities were clearly aware of Amadar at the time, because they questioned him on arrival at the airport and began watching him then. When he was arrested in October, police raided his home and found traces of TNT, detonators, and other flammable substances. A search of the garbage outside his home found chemicals used to manufacture explosives. At the time of his arrest, intelligence indicated Amadar's targets included places associated with Israelis and Jews in Peru, including areas popular with Israeli backpackers, the Israeli embassy in Lima, and Jewish community institutions.

It warrants noting that Hezbollah activity in the Southern Hemisphere often includes links to the United States. This was underscored in January 2015 when the FBI's Miami field office released a "request for information" bulletin about a dual Venezuelan-Lebanese Hezbollah operative known both for raising money for the group and meeting with Hezbollah officials in Lebanon to discuss "operational issues."[24]

---

[19] Minister of Health Report on Smoking in Israel, 2015, page 54, http://www.health.gov.il/PublicationsFiles/smoking_2015.pdf

[20] Emanuele Ottolenghi and John Hannah. "To Combat Illegal Immigration, Trump Should Target Latin America's Hezbollah-Narco Nexus," *Foreign Policy*, December 23rd, 2016 http://foreignpolicy.com/2016/12/23/to-combat-illegal-immigration-trump-should-target-latin-americas-hezbollah-nacro-nexus/

[21] "Hezbollah has ties to Brazil's Largest Criminal Gang; Group also Found Active in Peru," Fox News Latino, November 11, 2014. http://latino.foxnews.com/latino/news/2014/11/11/hezbollah-has-ties-to-brazil-largest-criminal-gang-group-also-found-active-in/

[22] "Hezbollah has ties to Brazil's Largest Criminal Gang; Group also Found Active in Peru," Fox News Latino, November 11, 2014. http://latino.foxnews.com/latino/news/2014/11/11/hezbollah-has-ties-to-brazil-largest-criminal-gang-group-also-found-active-in/

[23] "Hezbollah has ties to Brazil's Largest Criminal Gang; Group also Found Active in Peru," Fox News Latino, November 11, 2014. http://latino.foxnews.com/latino/news/2014/11/11/hezbollah-has-ties-to-brazil-largest-criminal-gang-group-also-found-active-in/

[24] Federal Bureau of Investigation, Miami and San Diego Field Offices, "Seeking Information Ghazi Nasr al-Din," January 29, 2015. https://www.fbi.gov/wanted/terrorinfo/ghazi-nasr-al-din

Hezbollah today is more invested in operations in South America than ever before. Not only are counterterrorism officials tracking Hezbollah operational plotlines there on a regular basis, but one of the most prominent operatives behind the AMIA bombing has now risen up the ranks of the organization and is personally overseeing Hezbollah operations in the region.[25] Salman al-Reda, whose true name is reportedly Salman Raouf Salman, was the on-the-ground coordinator of the AMIA bombing. A dual Lebanese-Colombian citizen who lived at various times in Colombia, in Buenos Aires and in the Tri-Border area, al-Reda fled the region after the bombing, before being indicted by Argentine authorities for his role in the attack. But in the years that followed, he served as an active member of Hezbollah's Islamic Jihad Organization (IJO), the group's international terrorist apparatus, also known as the External Security Organization (ESO). He was especially active in Southeast Asia and South America in the 1990s, including a flurry of operational missions in 1997 with three visits to Panama, two to Colombia, and one to Brazil.[26] Following Mohammad Hamdar's arrest in Peru, he identified al-Reda as the Hezbollah operative who served as his handler and with whom he met with on three different occasions in Turkey to plan the Peru operation.[27]

Hezbollah's ties to certain governments in Latin America have been of particular concern. Of note, the current Vice President of Venezuela, Tareck al Aissami, was designated by the U.S. Treasury Department in February 2017 under a counter narcotics authority[28] and is also reportedly close to Hezbollah.[29]

Hezbollah's Foreign Relations Department

Alongside its clandestine foreign operatives and networks, Hezbollah also maintains a more public international presence through the Foreign Relations Department (FRD) representatives it maintains around the world. Sometimes referred to as Hezbollah's External Relations department, the FRD functions overtly in Lebanon and in a semi-public fashion abroad. Previously headed by Nawaf al-Musawi, the FRD is headed today by Ali Damush who added to the U.S. list of designated terrorists in January 2017.[30] Some FRD personnel stationed around the world are Lebanese sent abroad to perform these functions, while others are Hezbollah supporters who live in foreign countries and willingly perform this service for the group. Most have close ties to senior Hezbollah officials, and many have some military training themselves and personal ties to ESO officials as well. Around the world, Hezbollah FRD personnel provide logistics to visiting Hezbollah delegations and build "community centers" to engender support for Hezbollah within local Shia communities and serve as a base for the group's local activities. They also raise funds, spot potential recruits, and serve as liaison officials maintaining communications not only between local supporters and Hezbollah leaders in Lebanon but also among Hezbollah operatives around the world.

---

[25] Author interview with counterterrorism officials, June 9, 2015

[26] Author interview with counterterrorism officials, June 9, 2015

[27] Author interview with counterterrorism officials, June 9, 2015

[28] "Treasury Sanctions Prominent Venezuelan Drug Trafficker Tareck El Aissami and His Primary Frontman Samark Lopez Bello," U.S. Department of Treasury, February 13th 2017, https://www.treasury.gov/press-center/press-releases/Pages/as0005.aspx

[29] Emanuele Ottolenghi, "Meet Venezuela's New VP, fan of Iran and Hezbollah," The Hill, January 3, 2017, http://thehill.com/blogs/pundits-blog/international/314283-meet-venezuelas-new-vp-a-hezbollah-fan

[30] "State Department Terrorist Designations of Ali Damush and Mustafa Mughniyeh," U.S. Department of State, January 9. 2017, https://www.state.gov/j/ct/rls/other/des/266748.htm

FRD officials have long been active in South America and elsewhere around the world. In Africa, FRD official Ali Ahmed Chehade has coordinated travel for Hezbollah members and actively assists Abd al Menhem Qubaysi, who, according to U.S. government information, serves as a personal representative of Hezbollah leader Hassan Nasrallah in West Africa.[31] Qubaysi has also hosted senior Hezbollah officials visiting the Ivory Coast and elsewhere in Africa. His activities included speaking at Hezbollah events and opening an official Hezbollah foundation in the Ivory Coast which is used "to recruit new members for Hezbollah military ranks in Lebanon."[32] Such activities have drawn the attention of officials in Africa, where the regional body of the Financial Action Task Force (FAFT) noted Chehade's FRD activities in a report on terrorist financing in West Africa.[33] Elsewhere in Africa, the duties of FRD operatives Fouzi Fawaz and Abdallah Tahini included organizing Hezbollah delegations' visits to Nigeria.[34]

Hezbollah criminal enterprises run deep in Africa, as evidenced most recently by the arrest in Morocco, extradition, and indictment in Washington, D.C., of Hezbollah financier Kassim Tajideen.[35]

Iranian State Sponsorship

Of course, Hezbollah continues to enjoy significant financial and other support from Tehran. Beyond training, weapons and other kinds of support, Iran provides Hezbollah massive amounts of money, as exposed most recently in the February 2017 Treasury Department designation of Hasan Dehghan Ebrahimi, a Lebanon-based IRGC-Qods Force official. According to The Treasury Department, "Ebrahimi has facilitated cash transfers to Hezbollah worth millions of dollars," some of which was sent and laundered through the U.S.-designated Hezbollah construction firm al Wa'ad Company. Ebrahimi and some of his employees raised money and transferred and laundered funds through a network of Lebanon-based companies with ties across the region. [36]

Policy Options

There are several concrete steps that could be taken to strengthen current efforts to counter Hezbollah's ability to exploit the international financial system to its benefit:

---

[31] "Treasury Sanctions Hizballah Operatives in West Africa," U.S. Department of Treasury, June 11, 2013, http://www.treasury.gov/press-center/press-releases/Pages/jl1980.aspx
[32] "Treasury Target Hizballah Network in Africa," U.S. Department of the Treasury, May 27, 2009, http://www.treasury.gov/press-center/press-releases/Pages/tg149.aspx
[33] "Terrorist Financing in West Africa," Financial Action Task Force, Inter Governmental Action Group Against Money Laundering in West Africa, October 2013, http://www.fatf-gafi.org/publications/methodsandtrends/documents/tf-west-africa.html
[34] "Treasury Targets Africa- Based Hizballah Support Network," U.S. Department of the Treasury, February 26th, 2015, https://www.treasury.gov/press-center/press-releases/Pages/jl9982.aspx
[35] "Lebanese Businessman Tied to Hizballah Arrested For Violating IEEPA and Defrauding the U.S. Government," United States Department of Justice, March 24, 2017, https://www.justice.gov/usao-dc/pr/lebanese-businessman-tied-hizballah-arrested-violating-ieepa-and-defrauding-us-government
[36] "Treasury Sanctions Supporters of Iran's Ballistic Missile Program and Iran's Islamic Revolutionary Guard Corps – Qods Force," US Department of the Treasury, February 3, 2017, https://www.treasury.gov/press-center/press-releases/Pages/as0004.aspx

1. **Designate additional Hezbollah entities, as appropriate**. HIFPA proscribes doing business with designated Hezbollah entities, so the more Hezbollah entities included in Treasury and State department lists the more impactful the HIFPA legislation will be. While Lebanese regulatory authorities intervened to prevent so-called over-compliance with the U.S. law by local banks and forestall further confrontation with Hezbollah, additional U.S. designations of Hezbollah businessmen and businesses would give Lebanese banks cover to protect the Lebanese financial system from further abuse. This should include, but not be limited to, entities operating in Lebanon. Consider, for example, the list of Lebanese businesses designated along with Lebanon-based IRGC Qods Force operative Hasan Dehghan Ebrahimi in February 2017.[37]

   Targeting Hezbollah's criminal enterprises in South America, Africa and Europe would be important as well. Additionally, whenever possible, note the Hezbollah connections to Treasury or other actions taken under authorities other than support for terrorism, as in the case of the counter-narcotics action taken against the Waked Money Laundering Organization, so that these can be covered by HIFPA as well.

   Finally, consider follow on actions to existing designations, where appropriate. For example, Ebrahimi was providing Hezbollah funds through Hezbollah's al Waad construction firm, which was designated in 2009.[38] Similarly, Hezbollah's "Equip a Mujahid" social media fundraising campaign was launched by Hezbollah's Islamic Resistance Support Organization (IRSO), which was designated in 2006.[39] In fact, the Treasury Department revealed at the time that IRSO was raising funds for Hezbollah around the world using terms like "equipping a mujahid project."[40]

2. **Target key Hezbollah criminal support networks**. Hezbollah's Foreign Relations Department has taken on a variety of criminal and operational functions over the past few years and targeting its operatives and front organizations would deal a significant blow to the group.[41] Similarly, Hezbollah increasingly relies on the services provided by "super facilitators" who may not be Hezbollah members themselves but provide the group specialized services that are mission-critical for Hezbollah's criminal enterprises. Targeting these super facilitators would also be an effective way of undermining the group's ability to access and abuse the international financial system.[42] The arrest,

---

[37] "Treasury Sanctions Supporters of Iran's Ballistic Missile Program and Iran's Islamic Revolutionary Guard Corps –Qods Force," US Department of the Treasury, February 3, 2017, https://www.treasury.gov/press-center/press-releases/Pages/as0004.aspx

[38] "Treasury Targets Hizballah Construction Company, US Department of the Treasury, January 6, 2009, https://www.treasury.gov/press-center/press-releases/Pages/hp1341.aspx

[39] "Treasury Designated Key Hezbollah Fundraising Organization," US Department of the Treasury, August 29, 2006, https://www.treasury.gov/press-center/press-releases/Pages/hp73.aspx

[40] English translation of IRSO donation form including in Treasury's IRSO designation https://www.treasury.gov/resource-center/terrorist-illicit-finance/Documents/0829translationofreceipts.pdf

[41] Matthew Levitt, "Hezbollah's 'Diplomats' Go Operational," The Washington Institute, December 2nd, 2016, http://www.washingtoninstitute.org/policy-analysis/view/hezbollahs-diplomats-go-operational

[42] Matthew Levitt, "Hezbollah's Criminal Networks: Useful Idiots, Henchmen, and Organized Criminal Facilitators," The Washington Institute, October 2016, http://www.washingtoninstitute.org/policy-analysis/view/hezbollahs-criminal-networks-useful-idiots-henchmen-and-organized-criminal

extradition and forthcoming prosecution of designated Hezbollah financier Kassim Tajideen indicates a newfound willingness to target individuals or organizations that play key roles in Hezbollah's criminal support networks, and stands in stark contrast to the failure to secure the extradition of other arrested Hezbollah supporters around the world, such as the case of Ali Fayyad who was arrested in the Czech Republic but later released to Lebanon.

3. **Apply secondary sanctions under HIFPA to a financial institution banking Hezbollah or its associates outside the Middle East**, such as in Africa or Latin America. This would serve as a powerful reminder of HIFPA's global reach and minimize the impact on Lebanon's financial sector. Consider a financial institution like Balboa Bank & Trust, which was designated by the Treasury Department in the context of the action taken against the Waked Money Laundering Organization.[43]

4. **Revisit the question of designating Hezbollah as a Transnational Criminal Organization.** The outing of Hezbollah's Business Affairs Component resulted from a series of DEA cases run under the rubric of "Project Cassandra," which targeted "a global Hezbollah network responsible for the movement of large quantities of cocaine in the United States and Europe." But there are many other recent cases in which transnational organized criminal activities were carried out by people with formal, even senior ties to Hezbollah. Hezbollah's status as a transnational criminal organization (TCO) should be revisited.[44]

5. **Resume sanctioning Iran for state sponsorship of Hezbollah (and other) terrorism.** Hezbollah continues to receive significant funding and resources from Iran. Without undermining the Iran Deal, which is limited to nuclear development and proliferation, more vigorous action could be taken against entities such as the IRGC Qods Force, Mahan Air, and a host of other Iranian entities involved in Tehran's support for terrorism. The designation of Hasan Dehghan Ebrahimi in February 2017 was a move in the right direction.

6. **Enhance interagency coordination and cooperation against the Iran Threat Network (ITN).** All of the policy options laid out here require close interagency coordination and cooperation. In the past, that has been in short supply when it comes to dealing with Iran, Hezbollah and Tehran's other proxies. Today, organized Shia militias closely tied to Iran are operating in Iraq and Syria. These include Shia militants not only from Iraq and Lebanon, but from Pakistan, Afghanistan, the Gulf, and Africa. Designations and other interagency actions targeting ITN actors allied with Hezbollah would go a long way toward undermining some of Hezbollah's key allies. The ITN threat is growing, not shrinking, and demands maximum coordination between the intelligence community, law enforcement, regulatory bodies and policy departments and agencies. One positive sign in this regard is the use of convening bodies such as the

---

[43] "Treasury Sanctions the Waked Money Laundering Organization." U.S. Department of the Treasury, May 5th. 2016, https://www.treasury.gov/press-center/press-releases/Pages/jl0450.aspx

[44] Matthew Levitt, "Hezbollah's Transnational Organized Crime," The Washington Institute, April 21st, 2016, http://www.washingtoninstitute.org/policy-analysis/view/hezbollahs-transnational-organized-crime

Global Counterterrorism Forum (GCTF) and the Law Enforcement Coordination Group (LECG) to address best practices for countering Hezbollah's terrorist, criminal and other illicit activities.[45]

---

[45] Matthew Levitt, "America May Have Unlocked a Key to Fighting Terrorism—and It Doesn't Involve Drones," The Washington Institute, January 8th, 2016. http://www.washingtoninstitute.org/policy-analysis/view/america-may-have-unlocked-a-key-to-fighting-terrorism-and-it-doesnt-involve; and "Treasury Hosts Meeting of the Law Enforcement Coordination Group Focused on Countering Hizballah's Terrorist Activities," U.S. Department of the Treasury, May 8th, 2017, https://www.treasury.gov/press-center/press-releases/Pages/sm0075.aspx

Chairman ROYCE. Thank you. Mr. Asher.

STATEMENT OF DAVID ASHER, PH.D., MEMBER, BOARD OF DIRECTORS, CENTER ON SANCTIONS AND ILLICIT FINANCE, FOUNDATION FOR DEFENSE OF DEMOCRACIES

Mr. ASHER. Chairman Royce, Ranking Member Deutch, and other members of the Foreign Affairs Committee, thanks for the opportunity to discuss with you the challenges we face countering Hezbollah's rapidly expanding global web of terror, crime, and insurgency, including its direct ties to the United States.

I will be brief about the challenges we face in combating Lebanese Hezbollah's illicit web of activities and finances, and begin with a little recounting of how I got involved. Beginning in 2008, in the summer, I had the honor of advising the man on my left and several others in the room at the Drug Enforcement Administration and the Department of Treasury, Special Operations Command, Department of State, and Customs Border Protection on developing and spearheading a unified strategy across law enforcement and special operations to pursue Hezbollah's web of activities, with the goal of fundamentally disrupting Hezbollah's growing involvement in cocaine trafficking and money laundering, including through the United States financial system and through our own borders.

I am proud to say that a seamless collaborative web of combining a small group of U.S. agencies was established and leveraged to combat these activities using every agency's unique authority. So it is a whole-of-government approach that makes you proud about being part of this government. It is a combination of law enforcement, financial, criminal, civil, and regulatory authorities that led to a wide range of actions that you have heard about, providing a framework to deter, disrupt, and publicly illuminate the global illicit Hezbollah network. I think it was probably the most successful operational effort taken against Hezbollah to date by the U.S. Government after many years of inaction.

Yet, in the last years of the previous administration, for reasons that most definitely had to do with the Iran deal and concerns of interfering with it, which I thought were totally unfounded as a former nuclear negotiator with Iran and North Korea, we lost much of the altitude that we had gained in our global effort. And many aspects—including key personnel who were reassigned, budgets that were slashed, and many key elements of the investigations that were underway—were undermined. And it was a bit of a tragedy and a travesty. And I think it was, again, very unfounded. But today, we have to deal with the legacy of that and how to rebuild this capability, knowing that you can have a nuclear deal with Iran and you can contain and disrupt its illicit activities and terrorist activities, and we really have to do both.

But the result today is that criminal states and criminal terrorist organizations continue to benefit from a type of implicit immunity from prosecution. And Mr. Royce, you and I have gone over this with North Korea over the years. We still haven't seen the types of charges that were assembled against that government, even in the wake of the Sony attacks, and more recently, hacking of the Federal Reserve Bank in New York. Moreover, neither al-Qaeda nor Hezbollah has ever been organizationally prosecuted by the Department of Justice for repeatedly attacking the United States, killing thousands, or hundreds, of our citizens, and for being tied to a wide range of transnational organized crimes and violations of our laws. And by the way, the same is true with the Islamic State, of which I had the honor to be the Deputy Special Coordinator on the economic warfare side at the State Department a couple years ago.

We have not applied Mafia-style RICO prosecutions that would aim to incarcerate the members of these organizations for life, take away their sanctuaries, strip them of their finances, and undermine their credibility. I, frankly, have no good answer why, except that I have heard from people, including Director Comey, that there is a sense of fear that if we do this, it is going to lead to reprisals.

I personally spearheaded the targeting of a Lebanese Canadian bank, a $5½ billion bank that was at the heart of Hezbollah and Iran's finances in Lebanon. We did not receive retaliation as a nation for bankrupting their largest financial institution. I think the fears are overwrought, and I find the phobias surrounding prosecution of terrorists baseless, bizarre, and moreover, largely against the spirit in the letter of the laws we are sworn to uphold.

Today, I would like to highlight that the Department of Justice needs to rebuild, properly fund, and expand capabilities and investigations against what I call the Iran action network, not just the threat network: Hezbollah's terrorist and military wing and their friends and partners in criminal states like Venezuela and North Korea.

And indeed, we can discuss this if you would like. The level of cooperation between the Government of Venezuela, the Government of Iran, the Government of Syria, and Lebanese Hezbollah that we observed in undercover operations with which we personally were involved, including people in this room, was absolutely astonishing. The evidentiary basis to take down this entire global network exists. The facts are clear, and they are already revealed in many unsealed indictments.

Thank you for your time and I look forward to any questions you have.

[The prepared statement of Mr. Asher follows:]

House Foreign Affairs Committee

Attacking Hezbollah's Financial Network:
Policy Options

DAVID ASHER, PH.D.

Board of Advisors
Center on Sanctions and Illicit Finance
Foundation for Defense of Democracies

Washington, DC
June 8, 2017

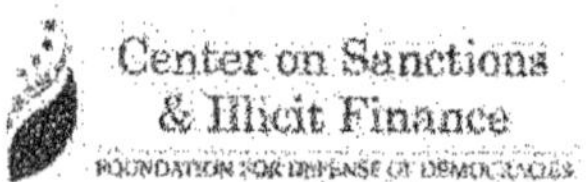

Center on Sanctions
& Illicit Finance
FOUNDATION FOR DEFENSE OF DEMOCRACIES

www.defenddemocracy.org/csif

David Asher   June 8, 2017

Chairman Royce, Ranking Member Engel, and other members of the Foreign Affairs Committee, I thank you for the opportunity to testify on this important topic of U.S. and international efforts to counter Hizballah's global network of terror, crime, and resistance, including its direct ties to the United States.

I will be brief about the challenge we face, touch on the strategy I helped the previous administration develop against Hizballah's illicit activities and finances, and then propose where we need to go next to achieve a long sought, but so far unattained, strategic effect against this pernicious, but highly capable, criminal resistance and terrorist organization and its state sponsors and partners.

- Over the last decade, Lebanese Hizballah has morphed from being a terrorist organization and politico-military (pol-mil) resistance movement to becoming a transnational criminal terrorist resistance organization fueled by a large and global illicit financial and business apparatus.
- Hizballah's drugs-for-intelligence program has evolved into a massive drugs-for-profit initiative.
- Hizballah, partnered with Latin American cartels and paramilitary partners, is now one of the largest exporters of narcotics from South and Central America to West Africa into Europe and is perhaps the world's largest money laundering organization.
- Organized crime—ranging from cocaine and heroin trafficking to selling counterfeit currency and cigarettes, along with massive money laundering via the Lebanese banking system—has become a much larger source of funding for Hizballah than support from Iran.
- Hizballah's External Security Organization (*i.e.* its terrorist wing) uses crime for exporting its influence, increasing followers around the world, and generating income.
- Defending against, attacking, and defeating Hizballah's growing military capacity requires defending against, attacking, and defeating its global financial and facilitation network.
- We built the means to do this but for reasons that remain mysterious, elusive, and hard to comprehend, much of what we built was willfully scrapped toward the end of the previous administration.
- Rebuilding this capacity and strategy will require significant resourcing, prioritization, and oversight by this Committee.

Beginning in the summer of 2008, I had the honor of advising the Drug Enforcement Administration, Department of the Treasury, Special Operations Command, Department of State, and Customs and Border Protection on developing and spearheading the implementation of a strategy to pursue Hizballah's web of illicit activities and finances, focusing on Hizballah's rapidly expanding involvement in cocaine trafficking and money laundering of the proceeds.

Our joint strategy contained the following key elements:
- **Use evidence from criminal investigations to support designations as well as make criminal cases.**

- **Pursue the narco-traffickers**—DEA Operation Titan (Colombia La Oficina De Envigado partnership with Hizballah); Project Cassandra (Hizballah global cocaine trafficking network under the Islamic Jihad); and Operation Perseus targeting Venezuela Cartel de Soles, "Los Turkos" and the Chavez regime's partnership with Hizballah, Iran, and Syrian governments (Conviasa flights from Venezuela to Syria and Iran, onward shipments to Europe)
- **Pursue the narco-money launderers:** Designation of Ayman Joumaa, Ali Kharroubi, the Ellissa Group, and the Hassan Ayash Exchange House under Drug Kingpin Act (Jan 2011). Join forces with CBP and FBI.
- **Pursue the bankers:** Designation of LCB as "a primary money laundering concern" under section 311 of the USA PATRIOT act (February 2011)
- **Pursue the used car money laundering scheme:** $483 million SDNY IEEPA forfeiture complaint against LCB, Hizballah, and the used car "dirty thirty" (December 2011)
- **Seize and forfeit financial assets: USC 18-981K strategy**
- **Use USA Patriot Act Section 311 against exchange houses** (Halawi/Rmeity)
- **Pursue the kingpins, Super Facilitators, and the Islamic Jihad Organization plus government partners under the Racketeer Influenced Corrupt Organizations Act (RICO) (2012- present)**

A seamless collaborative effort combining a small group of U.S. agencies was established and then leveraged to combat Hizballah utilizing each agency's unique authorities. This combination of law enforcement's criminal, civil, and regulatory authorities led to actions that provided a framework to deter, disrupt, and publicly illuminate Hizballah's global illicit network. The result was the most successful path taken against Hizballah to date. Yet success was undermined just as it was occurring, perhaps because of fear of the consequences. For a very low financial cost we could have legally taken apart the finances, the global organization, and the ability of Hizballah to readily terrorize us, victimize us, and run a criminal network through our shores, inside our banking system, and—in partnership with the world's foremost drug cartels—target our state and society. Instead, in narrow pursuit of the P5 + 1 agreement, the administration failed to realize the lasting effect on U.S. law enforcement collaborative efforts and actively mitigated investigations and prosecutions needed to effectively dismantle Hizballah and the Iran "Action Network". Senior leadership presiding, directing, and overseeing various sections within the Department of Justice, Department of Homeland Security, Department of State, and portions of the U.S. Intelligence Community systematically disbanded any internal or external stakeholder action that threatened to derail the administration's policy agenda focused on Iran. Top law enforcement officers working Hizballah, Iran, and Venezuela cases were reassigned from key investigative units and moved to peripheral assignments. Several top cops retired. Frankly, it was a mix of tragedy and travesty combined with a seriously misguided turn of policy that resulted in no real strategic gain and a serious miscarriage of justice.

The result is that criminal states and criminal terrorist organizations continue to benefit from a type of implicit immunity from prosecution. Neither al-Qaeda nor Hizballah has ever been organizationally prosecuted for repeatedly attacking the United States, killing our citizens, and for being tied to a wide number of trans-national organized crimes in violation of our laws. The same is true with the Islamic State. Despite clear and abiding bodies of evidence and testifying witnesses, these terrorist organizations have, in effect, been shielded from mafia-style RICO prosecutions that would aim to incarcerate their members for life, take away their sanctuary, strip them of their finances, and undermine their credibility. I have even heard statements of fear of reprisal should these terrorists be prosecuted from top DOJ officials as well as senior law enforcement agency leaders and intelligence analysts. I personally find this phobia, baseless, bizarre, and, moreover, against both the spirit and the letter of the laws we are sworn to uphold.

Today I am confident all of this is coming to an end. We have a White House and NSC determined to attack and defeat not only the Islamic State and al-Qaeda but also take on Iran and Hizballah terrorist networks, finances, facilitators, and senior functionaries. We have a superb and determined National Security Advisor who believes in the power of strategic law enforcement, the most knowledgeable and capable NSC Middle East team in history, and a new NSC Trans-National Threats Directorate that is ably run and mandated to take on narco-terrorism, criminal states, and counter threat finance and facilitation networks globally.

However, even with a proper policy and strategy in place, we need to see actions—and lots of them—synched together in a coherent and effective campaign strategy. The capabilities and capacities of the Department of the Treasury, intelligence community, and special operations community to inflict economic damage, infiltrate and undermine adversarial networks, states, and organizations must be broadened, deepened, and bolstered. The FBI, ICE, Customs and Border Protection, and the Secret Service must not only find, foil, and put down terrorist plots, they need to tackle entire networks and organizations. Our Department of Justice must rebuild, properly fund, and expand capabilities and investigations against the Iran "Action Network," Hizballah's terrorist and military wing, and their friends and partners in the leadership of the criminal governments of Venezuela and North Korea. Our prosecutors must be prepared to use tools like RICO to indict these terrorists' networks from foot to toe and tail to tooth, aiming to destroy them, bankrupt them, and lock up their leaders for life. I also have hope that the State Department will not be stripped of its resources and mandate for counter-threat finance and law enforcement but rather refocus its efforts to actively carry out economic and political "warfare" as an alternative to actual war. Finally—and critically—we need an overarching counter Hizballah USG task force, with intel agencies supporting law enforcement agencies (not opposing them) and evidence gathered, shared, and used coherently by all the investigators (including the FBI). This task force would support a unified prosecution strategy among all the different US Attorney's offices and the DOJ writ-large.

In closing, I have great hope that this administration has the capacity and strategy to effectively take on Lebanese Hizballah and its partners in crime but there is much work to do and no time to wait. Thanks to this Committee for its tremendous support on legislative mandates and resources.

I ask that the rest of my remarks be submitted for the record.

Timeline of the Iran-Hizballah Super Facilitator Initiative

- January 26, 2011: Foreign Narcotics Kingpin Designation, U.S. Department of Treasury, Office of Foreign Asset Control (OFAC): JOUMAA Drug Trafficking and Money Laundering Organization. The U.S. Department of the Treasury's Office of Foreign Assets Control (OFAC) designated **(NON USPER)** Lebanese narcotics trafficker Ayman JOUMAA, as well as nine **(NON USPER's)** individuals and 19 entities connected to his drug trafficking and money laundering organization as Specially Designated Narcotics Traffickers (SDNTs) pursuant to the Foreign Narcotics Kingpin Designation Act (Kingpin Act). Financial companies designated were the Hassan Ayash Exchange Company, the Ellissa Exchange Company, and New Line Exchange Trust Co. OFAC also targeted Hassan AYASH, Hassan Mahmoud AYACHE, Jamal Mohamad KHAROUBI, Ali Mohammed KHARROUBI, Ismael Mohammed YOUSSEF, and Ziad Mohamad YOUSSEF for their roles in these money exchanges. Ali Mohammed KHARROUBI owns Ellissa Holding, which was designated. Ellissa Holding controlled nine companies in Lebanon, Benin, and the Democratic of Congo, including Ellissa Group SA, the subsidiary of Ellissa Holding in Benin involved in the sale of used cars in Africa.

- February 10, 2011: **U.S. Department of Treasury, Financial Crimes Enforcement Network (FinCEN) public announcement that the Lebanese Canadian Bank SAL and subsidiaries has been identified under the U.S. Patriot Act Section 311 as a financial institution of primary money laundering concern.** Hizballah's $5.5 billion main bank was thrown into crisis, suffering several billion dollars in runs on deposits.

- November 3, 2011: **(NON USPER)** Ayman JOUMAA Criminal Indictment in the United States Eastern District of Virginia (EDVA). True Bill: Cocaine conspiracy, money laundering conspiracy, and criminal forfeiture proceedings.

- December 15, 2011: **The United States Attorney's Office (USAO) in the Southern District of New York (SDNY) filed a civil money laundering and forfeiture complaint seeking $483 million dollars from entities including the Lebanese Canadian Bank, exchange houses, and car dealers that facilitated a Hizballah-related money laundering scheme through the United States.**

- December 29, 2011: The U.S. Department of the Treasury's Office of Foreign Assets Control (OFAC) designated **(NON USPER's)** Lebanese-Colombian nationals Jorge Fadlallah CHEAITELLY ("CHEAITELLY") and Mohamad Zouheir EL KHANSA ("EL KHANSA") as Specially Designated Narcotics Traffickers (SDNTs) due to their significant role in international money laundering activities involving drug trafficking proceeds. OFAC also designated nine other individuals and 28 entities in Colombia, Panama, Lebanon, and Hong Kong with ties to CHEAITELLY and EL KHANSA. This action was taken pursuant to the Foreign Narcotics Kingpin Designation Act (Kingpin Act), prohibits U.S. persons from conducting financial or commercial transactions with these entities and individuals and freezes any assets the designees may have under U.S. jurisdiction.

- June 24, 2012: **(NON USPER) Lebanese National** Nayef Mahmoud FAWAZ was arrested by Panamanian authorities pursuant to a DEA-issued provisional arrest warrant on drug trafficking and money laundering charges issued in the SDNY. **(NON USPER)** Rawson WATSON, a citizen of the United Kingdom, and **(NON USPER)** Nicolas EPSKAMP, a citizen of the Netherlands were also arrested as co-conspirators with FAWAZ for conspiring to transport over $30 million dollars' worth of cocaine utilizing a U.S. registered aircraft. FAWAZ pled guilty to the conspiracy and in addition also pled guilty to violating **International Traffic in Arms Regulations (ITAR)** and Export Administration Regulations (EAR) by procuring **Bell Helicopters for export to and on behalf of the Islamic Republic of Iran.**

- June 27, 2012: United States Treasury designation of **(NON USPER's)** Lebanese Nationals Abbas Hussein HARB and Ibrahim CHIBLI pursuant to the Kingpin Act for collaboration with designated drug kingpin Ayman JOUMAA in the movement of millions of dollars of narcotics-related proceeds. HARB's Colombia- and Venezuela-based organization laundered money for the JOUMAA network through the Lebanese financial sector. Chibli used his position as the manager of the Abbassieh branch of Fenicia Bank in Lebanon to facilitate the movement of money for both JOUMAA and HARB. Ali Houssein HARB (Abbas Hussein HARB's brother) and Kassem Mohamad SALEH (Ali Mohamad SALEH's brother) were also designated under the Kingpin Act for their links to the JOUMAA network. Ali Houssein HARB and Kassem Mohamad SALEH are dual citizens of Lebanon and Venezuela.

- June 27, 2012: The U.S. Department of the Treasury designation of Lebanese Colombian national Ali Mohamad SALEH pursuant to E.O.13224 as a Specially Designated Global Terrorist for acting for or on behalf of and providing financial, material, or technological support to Hizballah. He is a former Hizballah fighter with knowledge of Hizballah operations plans due to his contact with Hizballah authorities in Lebanon. He was previously designated under the Kingpin Act on December 29, 2011, for his role as a Macau based money launderer for the CHEAITELLY/EL KHANSA criminal organization, which is linked to the JOUMAA network.

- August 20, 2012: **The USAO SDNY conducted a forfeiture action on the Societe Generale Banque au Libon (SGBL) accounts that contained $150 Million Dollars from the sale of the Lebanese Canadian Bank which were**

held at Banque Libano Francaise (BLF). The seizure and forfeiture action utilized statutes of U.S. Law pursuant to Section 981 (K) and was attributed to the December 15, 2011 filed complaint by the USAO SDNY.

- October 2012: The December 15, 2011 $483 million dollar SDNY filed civil money laundering and forfeiture complaint was amended to include specific information that outlined Hizballah's Drugs for Intelligence Program. This amendment added judicially obtained criminal evidence that revealed Hizballah members located in the Dahiya neighborhood of Beirut, Lebanon discussed trafficking cocaine in Europe and expressed interest in developing transnational cocaine transport routes to Europe and Africa. The Hizballah member's explained that Hizballah had used cocaine as part of a drugs for intelligence program to buy intelligence about Israel.

- April 23, 2013: U.S. Department of Treasury, FinCEN public announcement that identified the Kassem Rmeiti & Company for Exchange and the Halawi Exchange Company co-located in Lebanon along with their respective subsidiaries under the U.S. Patriot Act Section 311 as a financial institution of primary money laundering concern.

- September 24, 2013: The Drug Enforcement Administration (DEA) in partnership with the US Special Operations Command, Customs and Border Protection, the Department of State, the United States Treasury, U.S. Federal Prosecutors, International Law Enforcement and judicial partners, formally began the Super Facilitator Initiative utilizing both criminal and civil resources to target the illicit narcotics trafficking in Europe, Latin America, West Africa and the Middle East. The initiative also focuses on the narcotics trafficking derived illicit financial flows that utilize existing External Security Organization (ESO) financial support units.

- April 5, **2014: Arrest of Lebanese National's (NON USPER's) Ali FAYYAD,** Faouzi JABER, and Khaled EL MEREBI **in Prague, Czech Republic pursuant to international weapons trafficking, drug trafficking, and money laundering charges issued by the USAO SDNY. FAYYAD is still a United States criminal fugitive wanted by the U.S. Department of Justice.**

- February 6, 2014: Arrest of Lebanese National **(NON USPER)** Ali El Delbi KOLEILAT in Brussels by the Belgian National Police pursuant to a U.S. Interpol Red Notice issued by DEA. KOLEILAT was arrested on a provisional arrest warrant based on charges of international drug trafficking and money laundering with judicial proceedings conducted by the USAO SDNY. KOLEILAT coordinated multi-ton shipments of cocaine and laundered narcotics proceeds globally. KOLEILAT was previously sanctioned by the United States Treasury for actions committed on behalf of the government of Liberia and Dictator **(NON USPER)** Charles TAYLOR.

- June 10, 2015: The U.S. Department of the Treasury designated Hizballah member **(NON USPER)** Adham TABAJA, his company Al-Inmaa Group for Tourism Works, and its subsidiaries, as well as Lebanese businessman **(NON USPER)** Kassem HEJEIJ and Hizballah Islamic Jihad member **(NON USPER)** Husayn Ali FAOUR who provide support and services to Hizballah. Car Care Center, a front company based in Lebanon that supports Hizballah's transportation needs was also designated. Treasury's actions against these three individuals and four companies were taken pursuant to Executive Order (E.O.) 13224, which targets terrorists and those providing support to terrorists or acts of terrorism.

- July 29, 2015: Arrest of Lebanese National **(NON USPER) Ali Hassan MANSOUR arrested** pursuant to a provisional arrest warrant issued in the USAO Southern District of Florida by French authorities through diplomatic channels. MANSOUR was charged with multiple counts of money laundering over the course of a narcotics conspiracy. MANSOUR a large-scale money launderer based in Beirut, Lebanon, who operates on six continents and launders hundreds of millions of dollars annually. Mansour is also a key money launderer and drug trafficker for the Lebanese Hizballah (LH), External Security Office, and Business Affairs Component (BAC) global illicit network.

- October 1, 2015: The U.S. Department of the Treasury's Office of Foreign Assets Control (OFAC) designated **(NON USPER's)** four Lebanese and two German nationals and 11 companies as Specially Designated Narcotics Traffickers pursuant to the Foreign Narcotics Kingpin Designation Act (Kingpin Act). These individuals provide support for narcotics trafficking and money laundering activities conducted by Lebanese-Colombian drug trafficker and money launderer Ayman Saied JOUMAA, key JOUMAA associate **(NON USPER)** Hassan AYASH, and the JOUMAA criminal organization, which has ties to Hizballah. The action targets Lebanese national Merhi Ali ABOU MERHI who owns and controls the Abou Merhi Group, a holding company in Lebanon that is also designated today. Abou Merhi Group has multiple subsidiaries in Africa, the Middle East, and Europe including the following 10 designated companies: Abou-Merhi Lines SAL, a shipping line in Lebanon; Abou-Merhi Cruises (AMC) SAL, a travel agency in Lebanon; Le-Mall-Saida, a shopping mall in Lebanon; Queen Stations, a gas station in Lebanon; Orient Queen Homes, a real estate development in Lebanon; maritime shipping subsidiaries in Benin (Abou Merhi Cotonou), Nigeria (Abou Merhi Nigeria), and Germany (Abou Merhi Hamburg); Lebanon Center, a shopping mall in Jordan; and Abou Merhi Charity Institution in Lebanon.

- October 9, 2015: Arrest of **(NON USPER's)** Lebanese National's Iman KOBEISSI and Joseph ASMAR self-proclaimed Hizballah affiliate and associate on charges of laundering narcotics proceeds and international arms trafficking conspiring with a U.S. Department of State (DOS) Designated Foreign Terrorist Organization (FTO). The arrest warrants and indictments were conducted as a result of a DEA led investigation with judicial proceedings enacted by the USAO Eastern District of New York (ENDY).

- January 30, 2016: Arrest of Lebanese National **(NON USPER)** Ali KHALIFE in Bogota, Colombia by the Colombia National Police Special Investigations Unit (SIU) pursuant to a Drug Enforcement Administration (DEA) sealed Provisional Arrest Warrant (PAW) and sealed indictment issued by the U.S. Attorney's Office USAO SDNY. KHALIFE was arrested on U.S. Charges of engaging in a Cocaine Conspiracy and Money Laundering.

- January 24, 2016: **Operation Cedar enforcement raids occurred on January 24th and 25th, 2016 by law enforcement authorities in France, Germany, Italy, and Belgium, supported by DEA and CBP. These enforcement actions specifically targeted Lebanese Hizballah criminal operations in Europe.** 15 individuals involved in international criminal activities such as drug trafficking and drug proceed money laundering were arrested. During this series of raids across Europe 500,000 Euros in bulk cash, property in the form of 70 watches valued at $9 million (USD), weapons, one luxury vehicle and property valued at several million USD was seized. The seizure was a result of connecting assets in European via judicial proceedings to drug proceeds that were being collected by money launderers throughout Europe. The money was financing the same South American drug organizations that send cocaine shipments to the US. This action included support from Europol and Eurojust as well as law enforcement authorities in France, Germany, Italy, and Belgium. The following **(NON USPER's)** were arrested and are affiliated with or members of Hizballah, Mohammed NOUREDDINE (France Arrest), Mazen EL ATAT (France Arrest), Ali ZBEEB (France Arrest), Oussamah FAHS (France Arrest), Abdel MEHO (France Arrest), Elie SLIM (France Arrest)), Romanos KHATTAR (France Arrest)), Pierre NASSAR (France Arrest), Daniel KANDALAFT (France Arrest), Hassan TARABOLSI (Germany Arrest), Ali MANSOUR (Germany Arrest), Mohamed CHAHROUR (Germany Arrest), Hassan BERJAWI (Germany Arrest), Jamal KHALIL (Italy Arrest), and Maya KHALIL (Italy Arrest) Tarek BOUKAI (currently in the US was arrested in France upon his return), Adnan EL RAHI (currently in Angola- fugitive), Salwa ZBEEB (currently in Lebanon-fugitive), and Hassan BERJAWI (currently in Lebanon -fugitive).

- January 28, 2016: U.S. Department of the Treasury targeted Hizballah's financial support network by designating Hizballah-affiliated money launderers Mohamad NOUREDDINE and Hamdi ZAHER EL DINE, as well as Trade Point International S.A.R.L, a company owned or controlled by NOUREDDINE. NOUREDDINE and ZAHER EL DINE were designated to under Executive Order (E.O.) 13224 for providing financial services to or in support of Hizballah, which has long been designated by the U.S. as a terrorist organization. Trade Point International S.A.R.L. was designated for being owned or controlled by NOUREDDINE. Mohamad NOUREDDINE is a Lebanese money launderer who has worked directly with Hizballah's financial apparatus to transfer Hizballah funds via his Lebanon-based company Trade Point International S.A.R.L. and maintained direct ties to Hizballah commercial and terrorist elements. TABAJA operated in both Lebanon and Iraq. Hamdi ZAHER EL DINE is a Lebanese money launderer and employee of Trade Point International S.A.R.L., who has worked with Mohamad NOUREDDINE to transfer money for Adham TABAJA and Al-Inmaa Engineering and Contracting employees.

- February 1, 2016 **DEA and European Authorities Uncover Massive Hizballah Drug and Money Laundering Scheme (*7 countries involved in disrupting drug money flow for terror regime*). The Drug Enforcement Administration announced significant enforcement activity including arrests targeting Lebanese Hizballah's External Security Organization Business Affairs Component (BAC), which is involved in international criminal activities such as drug trafficking and drug proceed money laundering. These proceeds are used to purchase weapons for Hizballah for its activities in Syria.** This ongoing investigation spans the globe and involves numerous international law enforcement agencies in seven countries, and once again highlights the dangerous global nexus between drug trafficking and terrorism. This effort is part of DEA's Project Cassandra, which targets a global Hizballah network responsible for the movement of large quantities of cocaine in the United States and Europe. **This global network, referred to by law enforcement as the Lebanese Hizballah External Security Organization Business Affairs Component (BAC), was founded by deceased Hizballah Senior Leader Imad Mughniyah and currently operates under the control of Abdallah Safieddine and recent U.S.-designated Specially Designated Global Terrorist (SDGT) Adham Tabaja. Members of the Hizballah BAC have established business relationships with South American drug cartels, such as La Oficina de Envigado, responsible for supplying large quantities of cocaine to the European and United States drug markets.** Further, the Hizballah BAC continues to launder significant drug proceeds as part of a trade based money laundering scheme known as the Black Market Peso Exchange.

- May 5, 2016: U.S. Department of the Treasury Office of Foreign Asset Control (OFAC) designated the WAKED Money Laundering Organization (WAKED MLO) and its leaders, **(NON USPER)** Nidal Ahmed WAKED Hatum (WAKED Hatum) and **(NON USPER)** Abdul Mohamed WAKED Fares (WAKED Fares), as Specially Designated Narcotics Traffickers pursuant to the Foreign Narcotics Kingpin Designation Act (Kingpin Act). OFAC also targeted six WAKED MLO associates and 68 companies tied to the drug money laundering network, including Grupo Wisa, S.A., Vida Panama (Zona Libre) S.A., and Balboa Bank & Trust. Panamanian-Colombian-Spanish national WAKED Hatum and Panamanian-Lebanese-Colombian national WAKED Fares co-lead the WAKED MLO, which uses trade-based money laundering schemes, such as false commercial invoicing; bulk cash smuggling; and other money laundering methods, to launder drug proceeds on behalf of multiple international drug traffickers and their organizations.

- September 20, 2016: Arrest of (USPER) U.S. Citizen Mohammad AMMAR in Altadena, California by members of a combined State and Federal Task Force. AMMAR was arrested pursuant to a sealed State of Florida criminal indictment that includes charges of money laundering, wire fraud, and engaging in a narcotics conspiracy. AMMAR's role in the global network involved the illicit transnational movement of multi ton cocaine shipments along with a focus in the laundering of hundreds of millions of dollars on behalf of South American drug cartels. AMMAR specifically worked with the largest Colombian based drug cartel's, La Oficina de Envigado and Los Urabenos (AKA: Clan Usuga) AMMAR is a Colombia based Hizballah associated drug trafficker and money launderer.

- February 13, 2017: **U.S. Department of the Treasury's Office of Foreign Assets Control (OFAC) designated Venezuelan national** (NON USPER) **Tareck Zaidan EL AISSIMI MADDEH (EL AISSAMI) as a Specially Designated Narcotics Trafficker pursuant to the Foreign Narcotics Kingpin Designation Act (Kingpin Act) for playing a significant role in international narcotics trafficking. EL AISSAMI is the Executive Vice President of Venezuela.** EL AISSAMI 's primary front man, Venezuelan national **(NON USPER)** Samark Jose LOPEZ BELLO (LOPEZ BELLO), was also designated for providing material assistance, financial support, or goods or services in support of the international narcotics trafficking activities of, and acting for or on behalf of EL AISSAMI . OFAC further designated or identified as blocked property 13 companies owned or controlled by LOPEZ BELLO or other designated parties that comprise an international network spanning the British Virgin Islands, Panama, the United Kingdom, the United States, and Venezuela.

- March 13, 2017: **Arrest of Lebanese National (NONUSPER) Kassim Mohammad TAJIDEEN in Morocco pursuant to a U.S. Interpol Red Notice. TAJIDEEN was previously named as a prominent Hizballah member and money launderer and was designated by the United States Treasury in 2010. TAJIDDEN was arrested pursuant to a sealed indictment for Money Laundering, Wire Fraud, and International Emergency Economic Powers Act Statutes (IEEPA) pursuant to willfully violating U.S. Treasury Designations.** Belgian police previously arrested TAJIDEEN and his wife in a 2003 during a raid on Soafrimex, one of TAJIDEEN's Hizballah businesses in Antwerp. Belgian authorities accused TAJIDEEN and his wife of transferring "tens of millions of Euros" to Hizballah through his brother Ali, then a Hizballah commander.

Chairman ROYCE. Mr. Maltz.

STATEMENT OF MR. DEREK MALTZ, EXECUTIVE DIRECTOR, GOVERNMENTAL RELATIONS, PEN-LINK, LTD.

Mr. MALTZ. I would like to thank you for this opportunity to discuss this important topic. I retired from DEA, but I remain in daily contact with my colleagues and I pay close attention to the emerging threats to our country. I lost my brother Michael, U.S. Air Force para rescue early in the war and I am very passionate about national security and public safety issues. During the period I was the director of SOD, I had the privilege of working with numerous law enforcement agencies around the world, the intelligence community, and the Department of Defense. We had 30 agencies to include the U.K., Australia, Canada, NYPD, and we represented a center that was synchronizing efforts around the globe. I have witnessed the amazing results that have been achieved when agencies share operational intelligence and coordinate their efforts. Unfortunately I have also witnessed the lost opportunities that have been created when information wasn't shared.

In response to September 11th, very smart people in the government decided to form a counter-narco terrorism center inside the SOD operation. And they had vision because they knew the nexus between drugs and terrorism and crime was very, very closely tied, so the coordination became really important.

Over the years the nexus between crime and terror has grown. It is all about the money, they need money to operate. That is the bottom line. We heard from the experts that they are losing money, they are in bad financial shape, so drug trafficking is very important. We must shut down these funding streams, and we must use all the powerful tools of national power to attack this global threat. We can't investigate terrorism in a cocoon. The American public expects the government to cooperate and share information on these major threat investigations. And we must work very hard to break down the barriers that currently exist between those that investigate criminal groups, and those that are responsible for preventing terrorism. We need to develop a mutually supportive framework so the law enforcement actions can enhance intelligence community actions and vice versa, so intelligence community actions can enhance law enforcement actions.

I was the head of SOD when we started this initiative back in 2006, 2007 looking at global trade-based money laundering very, very alarming to me. I was fortunate to meet Admiral James Stavridis, the commander of SOUTHCOM, and he showed me a very disturbing visual that remains in my iPhone today, a fireball when narco terrorists and Islamic terrorists are joined; that is what I saw in my observations working on Project Cassandra, Operation Titan for almost 10 years. It was alarming that this decorated admiral had the vision back in those days to see what was evolving in South America with the drug traffickers.

Unfortunately, based on what I observed, this is what I see everyday in my mind, that fireball. Hezbollah, one of the worst terrorist organizations—killing all these Americans around the world—was laundering proceeds of cocaine through the Lebanese Canadian Bank. They were operating like a major drug cartel.

Now, in the press, we are hearing about the Captagon all over Syria. And I have some other information on that we can't discuss today.

Despite the limited support that our CNTOC task force received, we were very effective in what we were able to do. Project Cassandra was a long-term initiative target against a very significant organized crime network. We combined the resources and the expertise of some really, really smart people in the government from Treasury, CBP, and other agencies—including Dr. Asher and the lead agent in the back, Jack Kelly, who was the catalyst on this operation.

We were able to use the tools of national power to make a difference for our country's safety. And we went after this bank very hard, and we did a 311 action, we did civil actions with the Southern District of New York, and we actually seized $150 million from a bank account in Lebanon, because of really, really innovative and powerful laws of the United States. And you know what? They felt the pain because they tried to hide the money from us in LCB and they moved it to another bank, but we found it because we have some good investigators in this country. Thanks to the CNTOC task force, we actually ultimately forfeited $102 million, and it is in the U.S. asset forfeiture fund, so we are very proud of that.

Investigators documented $300 million moving into the U.S. from Lebanon for the purchase and the shipment of these cars to west Africa. There were 30 businesses named in this particular action. Unfortunately, and sadly, there are many more businesses operating that were not affected because of the lack of information sharing.

Although criminal law enforcement, the intelligence community, and others working on terrorism have come a long way in sharing information, there is a lot more to be done. At this point in this country's history, we don't need any more inspector general reports talking about lack of information sharing. We need some accountability on the people that aren't sharing. As state sponsorship of terrorism is fueled by drug trafficking, and criminal activities are on the rise, we have to pay more attention. The special operations division, within the Department of Justice, established itself as a multiagency coordination center that can immediately deconflict investigative information, coordinating operation and mitigating threats through its resources and its global capabilities.

I would highly recommend that this committee and other Members of Congress consider enhancing the special operations capabilities and designate it as the transnational organized crime center for America. It is critical, in my view, that we continue to use all the powerful laws and we continue to enhance the laws. There must be open and collaborative efforts between the criminal investigations and the intelligence community because we are in this together. We all are going to face the same consequences if we don't work together. We must illuminate the networks with the really smart people we have in America. We must use every tool and have an all-tools-available approach.

As the Senate report adequately and accurately depicted, the Lebanese Canadian Bank investigation served as a model for interagency success. I am excited and hopeful that the Department of

Justice and Homeland Security under the Trump administration will examine operations like Project Cassandra and pick out the best lessons learned and let us move forward.

Thank you for the opportunity to appear before you today. And I would like to discuss this important topic in any details. Thank you.

[The prepared statement of Mr. Maltz follows:]

UNITED STATES HOUSE OF REPRESENTATIVES
HOUSE COMMITTEE ON FOREIGN AFFAIRS

"ATTACKING HEZBOLLAH'S FINANCIAL
NETWORK: POLICY OPTIONS"

JUNE 8, 2017
STATEMENT OF DEREK S. MALTZ
INTRODUCTION

Chairman Royce, Ranking Member Engel and distinguished members of the committee, I would like to thank you for this opportunity to speak with you today regarding attacking Hezbollah's financial network and the dangerous connections between drug trafficking and terrorism. This topic has been a priority of mine while serving as the Special Agent in Charge (SAC), Drug Enforcement Administration (DEA), Special Operations Division (SOD) for almost 10 years. I have some recommendations and lessons learned to share as the new administration develops strategies to deal with this evolving and complex threat to the United States National Security.

I would also like to thank you for the continued support you provide DEA and the other law enforcement agencies in their efforts to address these complicated global threats. As the former Special Agent in Charge of the Special Operations Division, I had the privilege of working with numerous local, state, federal and international law enforcement agencies and have witnessed the amazing results that can happen when law enforcement, both our U.S. agencies and our foreign counterparts, share operational intelligence and coordinate efforts against our common enemies.

BACKGROUND:

Over the last 30 years, I have been honored to be an active participant of the Drug Enforcement Administration and now in the private sector to work with some of the best and brightest investigators. That being said, I'm very concerned that our collective efforts have some significant challenges as our agencies attempt to establish stronger counter threat finance operations against global terrorist organizations like Hezbollah. I will discuss a very successful operation of which I am highly familiar with. The investigation also known as Project Cassandra is a long term initiative targeting a very significant transnational organized crime organization. I have highlighted some investigative details within this document that demonstrates the amazing ability for the United States Government to disrupt, dismantle and destroy Transnational Organized Crime capabilities when agencies work in a unified fashion as opposed to compartmentalizing information and operations. I also included some recommendations.

In my 28 years in law enforcement, I've seen many operations that were both successful and failures. Many of the failures that I have witnessed were not a result of lack of effort or skill by the investigators. Rather, those failures were the result of lack of leadership and political infighting that created an environment built around securing and maintaining one's own kingdom, as opposed to serving the American people. I believe that if the U.S.G. would implement some of the ideas and philosophies in this document, we can make this country a safer place for current and future generations.

PROJECT CASSANDRA:

During 2004, Drug Enforcement Administration (DEA) agents in Miami initiated a large-scale money laundering investigation, titled Operation Titan. Operation Titan successfully used confidential sources to infiltrate a significant organized crime group in Medellin Colombian identified as the Oficina de Envigado. This very successful DEA investigation, coordinated by the Special Operations Division (SOD), a multi-agency operational coordination center with 30 agencies represented, led to unprecedented results and exposed elements of the Terrorist Group Hezbollah who were being funded by worldwide cocaine sales.

During this investigation several undercover activities were conducted which involved large sums of U.S. currency. As a result of the great investigative work, there was extensive intelligence developed on the main Colombia based organization and the Colombian National Police (CNP) initiated an investigation on the organization located in Colombia. Over a two-year period the CNP and DEA conducted an exceptional investigation and they identified a large scale Lebanese money launderer with activities connected with the Oficina de Envigado.

During 2008, the U.S. cooperative investigation with Colombia culminated with over 130 arrests, to include many of the senior-level operatives, and $23 million was seized. (Rotella, 2008) This case identified the scope and the alliance between South American drug traffickers to money laundering operations in Hong Kong, Central America, Africa and Canada, and a connection to several Lebanese criminals associated with a global organized crime network.

Based on the substantial information developed during Operation Titan and very alarming and emerging trends, the Counter-Narco Terrorism Operations Center (CNTOC) located at SOD commenced an initiative focusing on all aspects of this network. The CNTOC has representatives from numerous agencies to ensure that information collected and analyzed can be immediately passed to the appropriate agencies and that the agencies can work in a collaborative task force environment. The CNTOC spearheaded a focused investigation with the field offices on the Middle Eastern money launderers working with the South American drug traffickers who were shipping multi-ton quantities of cocaine into West Africa for distribution around the world. During this initiative, DEA identified the leader of this sophisticated network who coordinated multi-ton shipments of cocaine from Colombia to Los Zeta's Mexican Drug Cartel and was laundering hundreds of millions of dollars in drug proceeds back to Colombia. The main operative also established a very sophisticated network in West Africa to move currency via couriers back to Lebanon.

The CNTOC organized a four-phased plan to include OFAC designations against substantial targets, identified as Ayman Joumaa, Elissa and Ayash Exchange, a USA Patriot Act 311 action against Lebanese Canadian Bank, a civil money laundering action against Lebanese Canadian Bank and Hezbollah's used car businesses involved in the scheme and criminal prosecution directed at the leaders of the Hezbollah involved with the drug and money laundering operation. CNTOC's strategy included all the tools of national power in a focused effort to disrupt and dismantle this trade-based money-laundering scheme.

In January 2011, the Office of Foreign Assets Control (OFAC) of the Department of Treasury, under the specially designated narcotics traffickers kingpin program, designated ten individuals and twenty entities related to the Joumaa organization to include the Elissa and Ayash Exchanges in Lebanon. (Center, Treasury Targets Major Lebanese-Based Drug Trafficking and Money Laundering Network , 2011)

In February 2011, The Department of Treasury with DEA announced the identification of the Lebanese Canadian Bank (LCB) as a financial institution of primary money-laundering concern under section 311 of the USA Patriot Act. This was the first time ever the 311 Action was used in a drug case. The organized crime network was moving large shipments of drugs from South America to Europe and the Middle East via

West Africa and laundering hundreds of millions of dollars to accounts held at LCB as well as through trade base money-laundering involving consumer goods throughout the world, including used car dealerships in the U.S. LCB was helping Hezbollah through the Joumaa network. (Center, Treasury Identifies Lebanese Canadian Bank Sal as a "Primary Money Laundering Concern", 2011)

Subsequently in December 2011, there was a complaint filed in the Southern District of New York exposing this Lebanese money-laundering scheme which investigators documented over $300 million into United States for the purchase and shipment of used cars to West Africa. The complaint alleged that the assets of LCB, Hassan Ayash Exchange and Elissa Holding, along with the assets of approximately 30 U.S. car buyers and a U.S. shipping company and related entities that facilitate the scheme, are forfeitable as the proceeds of violations of the International Emergency Economic Powers Act (IEEPA). Through this investigation, the task force of agencies exposed the LCB as money-laundering for Hezbollah through a very aggressive financial attack against the network. The elaborate scheme exposed very innovative ways terrorist groups like Hezbollah could identify alternate sources of income to fund their operations. As terrorists are increasingly turning to criminal networks for their funding, this operation clearly supported this statement made by the President of the United States and Senior Homeland Security Officials. This particular complaint was seeking penalties totaling $483 million. From January 1, 2007 to early 2011 at least $329 million was transferred by wire from LCB and the two exchange houses and other financial institutions for the purchase and shipment of used cars. (DEA, DEA News: Civil Suit Exposes Lebanese, 2011)

One of the key elements identified during this investigation was the millions of dollars that were declared being transported across the Togo and Ghana border on its way from Benin to the airport in Accra where the cash was then be shipped by Middle East and couriers to Lebanon. When the cash arrived in Lebanon at Beirut airport, Hezbollah security safeguarded the delivery of the cash into the financial exchange houses. The money was then routed through the Lebanese Canadian Bank and other financial institutions and subsequently wire transferred to the United States so the used-car businesses can purchase vehicles. The vehicles were then shipped to West Africa for resale. It was estimated that the network would earn approximately 20% profit on each car that was sold. The DEA working with our partners at CBP also identified how the carparks in West Africa were exploding with volume.

During the same December time frame, the Eastern District of Virginia announced the indictment of Ayman Joumaa for coordinating the shipment of tens of thousands of kilograms of cocaine from Colombia to Los Zetas Drug Cartel for distribution into the United States over an eight year period. Joumaa was also charged with laundering millions of dollars in drug proceeds for the organization. Joumaa's organization was further exposed through the OFAC sanction. (EDVA, 2011)

Subsequent to the lawsuit against the LCB, investigators revealed that the LCB personnel moved assets to other banks in Lebanon in a way to hide the assets from the United States government. This criminal activity was part of the international scheme where several Lebanese financial institutions with connections to Hezbollah used the U.S. banks to launder narcotics proceeds through West Africa into Lebanon. In August 2012, the Southern District of New York filed a 981K action against five corresponding banks in the United States that were doing business with Banque Labano Francais. This particular Lebanese bank received $150 million from the Lebanese Canadian bank after they were exposed with their international money-laundering business. As a result of this very successful 981K action, the Banque Labano Francais, transferred $150 million to the United States Marshals Service account in New York. In June 2013, the Southern District of New York settled a civil forfeiture action against the Lebanese Canadian bank and the settlement required LCB to forfeit $102 million to the United States. This was an unprecedented action targeting Hezbollah and their worldwide illicit activities. The settlement also identified to the world that international money-launderers for terrorists and narco-traffickers will face serious consequences even when the activity is outside the US.(Justice, 2012) (York, 2013)

In April 2013, the Treasury Department along with DEA named two more Lebanese Exchange Houses, Kasim Remeiti and Halawi Exchange, as foreign financial institutions of primary money- laundering concern under section 311 of the USA Patriot Act. This was very significant since it was the first time the Treasury Department had used section 311 against a non-bank financial institution. These actions were all part of the ongoing DEA CNTOC strategy working closely with the Treasury Department to expose the businesses around the world working with the Joumaa organization. The significance of these actions is that it forces these financial institutions out of working in the US and international financial systems. These exchange houses used their money transmitting businesses to process millions of dollars on behalf of drug traffickers. Between 2008 and March 2011 Rmeti Exchange provided at least $25 million in payments to US based car dealerships and other exporters connected to Juma's organization. Halawi Exchange laundered profits from drug trafficking for a main Hezbollah official. In one year alone this business were engaged in multiple transfers over $4 million on behalf of one organization. (Center, Treasury Identifies Kassem Remeiti & Co. for Exchange and Halawi Exchange Co. as Financial Institutions of "Primary Money Laundering Concern", April)

Later in 2013, Rachel Louise Ensign, wrote in the Wall Street Journal, the Senators Call for Financial Sanctions on West Africa Drugs as part of a conclusion made in a report by Sen. Dianne Feinstein (D, Calif.), Chairman of the Caucus, and Sen. Chuck Grassley (R., Iowa) who is co- Chairman. The Senators called for financial sanctions targeting the West African drug trade in a new report. The bipartisan senate caucus on international narcotics control said the Treasury Department and other agencies should prioritize efforts to quash the flow of money linked to the growing drug trade in the region. Terrorist organizations in West and North Africa are in part financed by drug money, the report said. In recent years, a number of arrests in the region have exposed connections between the two, it said. The report hailed the U.S. government's 2011 lawsuit against the now-defunct Lebanese Canadian Bank, which alleged that the institution participated in a scheme that funded Hezbollah and involved cocaine sales in West Africa. The bank eventually settled for $102 million earlier this year. (Ensign, Senators Call for Financial Sanctions on West Africa Drugs, 2013)

The investigation began in 2006 and involved multiple agencies, including the Treasury Department and the U.S. Drug Enforcement Administration. **"The Lebanese Canadian Bank investigation and associated enforcement actions should serve as a model for future interagency cooperation," the report said.** Another suggestion was to prioritize by adding drug traffickers operating in the region to the Treasury Department's blacklist. A designation freezes a person's assets and generally prohibits Americans from engaging in business dealings with him or her. (Ensign, Senators Call for Financial Sanctions on West Africa Drugs - Wall Street Journal, 2013)

During February 2016, DEA working with European law enforcement identified a massive Hezbollah drug and money-laundering scheme. This complex investigation targeted Hezbollah's Lebanese Hezbollah's Business Affairs Component (LHBAC). This particular component has been engaged in weapons purchases for Hezbollah to support its activities in Syria. This investigation involved multiple countries and showed once again the connection between Hezbollah and drug trafficking. This particular aspect focused on LHBAC. The LHBAC formed a business relationship with the South American cocaine traffickers responsible for shipping multi-tons of cocaine around the world. The massive proceeds made by this element provides proceeds for the purchase of weapons needed for their international terrorist operations. (DEA, DEA and European Authorities Uncover Massive Hezbollah Drug and Money Laundering Scheme, 2016) During the entire initiative, DEA working with counterparts around Europe fully identified a very intricate network of couriers who were transporting millions of euros from Europe to the Middle East.

Building the Future:

One of my main recommendations to the new administration would be to take the foundation of what has been created at the CNTOC at the Special Operations Division with the several supporting intelligence centers and enhance the interagency efforts. After the U.S. Congress report on combatting drugs in West Africa rightfully concluded, **"The Lebanese Canadian Bank investigation and associated enforcement actions should serve as a model for future interagency cooperation"**. (Ensign, Senators Call for Financial Sanctions on West Africa Drugs, 2013). Now is the time for action and the U.S.G. should build on this success.

To illustrate the need for units such as CNTOC and added support from the new incoming leadership, one only needs to look at the December 19, 2016 article published by the Wall Street Journal titled, "The travels of Mrs. Murray's Toyota Unveils Terror-Finance Network". In this investigative article, the authors did a thorough job and reviewed the United States to Benin used car trade, which DEA and its partners had established, were involved in a global trade base money-laundering scheme to support Hezbollah's global operations. The WSJ concluded that the scheme is still operational and involved used-car businesses in the United States. The article goes on to describe the following disturbing facts:

- Many of the car dealers identified in the 311 initiative continued to ship cars to West Africa.
- The used-car export business to West Africa has expanded and is very active.
- The vehicle exports to Benin in 2015 totaled $434 million and were up from $47 million in 2005. (Christopher S. Stewart, 2016)

As we move into the future, identifying terrorist groups using criminal enterprises in order to fund and facilitate activities will continue to become increasingly more complex. The new leaders under President Trump must support and advance the multi-agency successful efforts of groups like the CNTOC. The United States Government also needs to continue its efforts to advance technical capabilities within law enforcement agencies.

I believe that by placing qualified personnel in key leadership positions with law enforcement background, we can ensure that communication is flowing appropriately in both directions between law enforcement and the other pertinent agencies. There are some reasonable and justified reasons to withhold information at times from key law enforcement personnel, but should be minimized. It would be my hope that we can improve those relationships by ensuring that law enforcement does not feel that they are "only a source of information" as opposed to a partner in the fight against terrorism. As terrorists are looking for funding to carry out their dangerous agendas, criminal activity has been a golden source of revenue. This means, the agencies need to "break down the barriers" and unite. In the year 2017, it's almost impossible to successfully investigate global terrorists without utilizing the amazing criminal law enforcement personnel around the globe. It should be "one great U.S.G. force". We need to unite not divide.

I am excited and hopeful that key Homeland Security and Justice Department personnel in the Trump administration will examine successful operations like the Lebanese Canadian Bank and Operation Titan and develop best practices moving forward. The complex transnational organized crime groups are constantly evolving and becoming more sophisticated. Law Enforcement and the Intelligence Community needs a sound strategy to continue to pursue the sophisticated groups and the U.S. Government needs a unified effort. They must place some of the best and brightest people into positions like the CNTOC and continue to pursue the sophisticated groups in a focused and prioritized manner. If you successfully crush a criminal organization's financial network, you will significantly increase the chances of disrupting their illicit activities.

Recommendations:

- SOD needs to be designated as the Transnational Organized Crime (TOC) Coordination Center for the USG and should be provided the necessary enhancements, support and directives from the highest levels of government to support President Trump's Executive Orders on Transnational Crime and Violent Crime. The SOD Center currently has over 30 agencies represented to include the NYPD, UK, Canada and Australia and has years of operational multi-agency successes of fighting TOC. The DOD and Intelligence Community also have participation and their equities are protected in the process.

- The basic principle that needs to be enforced to keep America safe is 100% Information sharing. The DOJ needs to maintain the leadership, oversight and responsibility for the multi-agency project since they are responsible for the ultimate prosecution. The Center needs to be adequately staffed. FBI and HSI should elevate the leadership within the center for maximum "unity of effort" and "buy in" from their field operatives and management.

- The DICE De-Confliction system, which is currently mandated by DOJ and DHS leadership, needs to be expanded to include the counter-terror investigations. The foundation has already been established. We also need the resources to ensure the DICE system is maintained, updated and refreshed.

- Since Crime and Terror overlap and we have identified several global fund raising schemes that are crossing into the criminal investigations, we need to break down the walls and legal impediments and develop sound sharing processes. Need to enhance the existing Global Threat Finance Teams with the expertise to disrupt and dismantle the financial aspects of these networks using all the powerful U.S. Treasury Actions.

- SOD has a robust International Investigations Program to go around the globe and take down huge threats working with our foreign counterparts around the globe. Since DEA has the largest worldwide presence of criminal investigators and years of experience working in the foreign arena, SOD, with input from all the agencies, is in a position to provide solid action plans on the highest level TOC targets.

- The leadership and command and control elements of the biggest threats to the United States are foreign and SOD has proven they can use the rule of law and obtain full cooperation from the counterparts to maximize the prosecutions in the United State.

References

Center, P. (2009, July 09). *Treasury Designates Medellin Drug Lord Tied to Oficina de Envigado Organized Crime Group*. Retrieved from Treasury.gov: https://www.treasury.gov/press-center/press- releases/Pages/tg201.aspx

Center, P. (2011, February 10). *Treasury Identifies Lebanese Canadian Bank Sal as a "Primary Money Laundering Concern"* . Retrieved from Treasury.gov: https://www.treasury.gov/press-center/press-releases/Pages/tg1057.aspx

Center, P. (2011, January 26). *Treasury Targets Major Lebanese-Based Drug Trafficking and Money Laundering Network* . Retrieved from Treasury.gov: https://www.treasury.gov/press-center/press-releases/Pages/tg1035.aspx

Center, P. (2012, June 27). *Treasury Targets Major Money Laundering Network Linked to Drug Trafficker Ayman Joumaa and a Key Hizballah Supporter in South America*. Retrieved from Treasury.gov: https://www.treasury.gov/press-center/press-releases/Pages/tg1624.aspx

Center, P. (April, April 23). *Treasury Identifies Kassem Rmeiti & Co. for Exchange and Halawi Exchange Co. as Financial Institutions of "Primary Money Laundering Concern"*. Retrieved from treasury.gov: https://www.treasury.gov/press-center/press-releases/Pages/jl1908.aspx

Christopher S. Stewart, R. B. (2016, December 19). *The Travels of Mrs. Murray's Toyota Unveil Terror-Finance Network*. Retrieved from wsj.com: http://www.wsj.com/articles/the-travels-of-mrs-murrays-toyota-unveils-terror-finance-network-1482163526

DEA. (2011, Dec 15). *DEA News: Civil Suit Exposes Lebanese* . Retrieved from DEA.gov: https://www.dea.gov/pubs/pressrel/pr121511.html

DEA. (2016, February 01). *DEA and European Authorities Uncover Massive Hizballah Drug and Money Laundering Scheme*. Retrieved from dea.gov: https://www.dea.gov/divisions/hq/2016/hq020116.shtml

EDVA. (2011, December 13). *U.S. Charges Alleged Lebanese Drug Kingpin with Laundering Drug Proceeds for Mexican and Colombian Drug Cartels*. Retrieved from Justice.gov: https://www.justice.gov/archive/usao/vae/news/2011/12/20111213joumaanr.html

Ensign, R. L. (2013, December 12). *Senators Call for Financial Sanctions on West Africa Drugs*. Retrieved from wsj.com: http://blogs.wsj.com/riskandcompliance/2013/12/12/senators-call-for-financial-sanctions-on-west-africa-drugs/

Ensign, R. L. (2013, December 12). *Senators Call for Financial Sanctions on West Africa Drugs - Wall Street Journal*. Retrieved from feinstein.senate.gov: https://www.feinstein.senate.gov/public/index.cfm/feinstein-in-the-news?ID=45858A0D-A037-4C55-A2D6-B7AEDAF357E7

Justice. (2012, August 20). *Manhattan U.S. Attorney Announces Seizure Of $150 Million In Connection With A Hizballah-Related Money Laundering Scheme*. Retrieved from Justice.gov: https://www.justice.gov/archive/usao/nys/pressreleases/August12/lcbseizure.html

Rotella, C. K. (2008, October 22). *LA Times.com*. Retrieved from Drug probe finds Hezbollah link: http://articles.latimes.com/2008/oct/22/world/fg-cocainering22

York, S. D. (2013, June 25). *Manhattan U.S. Attorney Announces $102 Million Settlement Of Civil Forfeiture And Money Laundering Claims Against Lebanese Canadian Bank*. Retrieved from Justice.gov: https://www.justice.gov/usao-sdy/pr/manhattan-us-attorney-announces-102-million-settlement-civil-forfeiture-and-money

Chairman ROYCE. Thank you, Mr. Maltz. Thank you for your service.

Dr. Karlin.

STATEMENT OF MARA KARLIN, PH.D., ASSOCIATE PROFESSOR OF PRACTICE AND ASSOCIATE DIRECTOR OF STRATEGIC STUDIES, SCHOOL FOR ADVANCED INTERNATIONAL STUDIES, JOHNS HOPKINS UNIVERSITY

Ms. KARLIN. Chairman Royce, Mr. Deutch and members of the committee, thank you for this opportunity to appear before you today. Having examined Hezbollah as a national security policy-maker and a researcher for nearly two decades, I can confidently say this is a critical time to assess it. To effectively examine Hezbollah's financing, one must consider the political military context, particularly the impact and implications of the Syria conflict. Hezbollah has both benefited from and suffered because of its involvement there. Starting with the latter, support around the region has been shaky, as Sunnis around the Middle East watch Hezbollah aid in Syria's destruction. In Lebanon, the Shia see body bags of its youth. With estimates of 5,000 to 10,000 Hezbollah members fighting in Syria, it is hemorrhaging members like never before. Indeed, it has bled more in Syria than in fighting Israel, over a much shorter period of time. Hezbollah is waging a counterinsurgency to prop up Assad. The American military has learned, over the last decade and a half, that this type of conflict is extremely difficult and costly in blood and in treasure. Notable power shifts are at play because of the Syria conflict. The Assad regime owes its continued existence to Hezbollah. Meanwhile, Hezbollah has become a regional player—it has a substantial presence in at least four different countries—but is increasingly exerting Iran's mandate.

Today, Qassem Soleimani is the decider of Hezbollah's future, not Hassan Nasrallah. The conflict in Syria shifted the dynamics between them such that Hezbollah seems willing to do whatever Iran wants, whenever it asks, and regardless of the cost. Iran is willing to fight until the last Hezbollah member in Syria, and it appears Hezbollah is, too; that is a problem for Hezbollah. Lebanon Shia are isolated, increasingly disillusioned by Hezbollah, but see few protectors. Many of those now joining Hezbollah focus on money. Indeed, one out of every four Lebanese Shia receives a salary from Hezbollah. Given this, the Lebanese Shia desperately need alternative, political representation and new opportunities, particularly in the economic sector.

Now to be sure, Hezbollah has benefited from its involvement in the Syrian conflict. Ten years ago, I was most worried about Hezbollah's weapons, now I am more worried about the experience Hezbollah has gained. Before it was a capable military force, good at a limited number of missions. Its portfolio has expanded dramatically. It has become a hardened force, adept at facilitating Iranian power projection around the Middle East. It has learned to command and control a complicated conflict in collaboration with numerous actors. It has acquired substantial experience in diverse environments, using increasingly sophisticated weapons. And as the operating space in Syria becomes crowded, and the U.S. military deepens its direct involvement there, we could see inadvertent or deliberate interactions with Hezbollah.

Now turning to Lebanon. While the situation appears quiet, one should not be fooled. For a country of a few million brimming with sizable populations of long-term Palestinian refugees, and more recent Syrian ones, and 18 or so different confessional groups, it is a miracle Lebanon exists. That is important to remember—the state has institutions, but they are fragile. They do little in the way of actual governing, and are often beholden to nonstate forces or external actors.

As you all know well, Lebanon's military is a top recipient of U.S. security assistance. It is in U.S. interests for the military to fight nefarious actors whenever it is willing. Without U.S. support, its ability to do so is minimal. It has deployed throughout much of Lebanon and taken important, albeit insufficient, steps to counter violent actors. The Lebanese military is flawed, but it is nationally supported and well-respected in a country with few institutions that can be described as such. It has an impeccable record of maintaining control over its weapons over the last decade. And, of course, Hezbollah does not need the Lebanese military's weapons. It has Tehran and Damascus for that. Hezbollah poses the most potent threats to Lebanon's internal security. It turned its weapons on the Lebanese people in 2008 and will do so again if necessary.

There is a memorial to the civil war at the front of Lebanon's ministry of defense composed of weapons collected from various groups melted together. You will not, however, find Hezbollah stockpile in that hunk of resting metal.

As you seek to legislate further action against Hezbollah, I urge you to ask the following questions: To the White House, is the strategy focused on ISIL or does it include the Assad regime? To the intelligence community, how are Iran, Syria, and Russia adjusting their support for and/or collaboration with Hezbollah and Syria? What points of friction exist between them and Hezbollah? Can they be exploited? And what about between the Lebanese Shia and Hezbollah? To the State and Defense Departments, how are they regularly assessing their program to strengthen the Lebanese military? And to the Defense Department, how is the U.S. military accounting for the increased potential of U.S.-Hezbollah confrontation in and around Syria? Thank you very much.

[The prepared statement of Ms. Karlin follows:]

Testimony of Mara Karlin, Ph.D.
Associate Professor of Practice and Associate Director of Strategic Studies,
The Paul H. Nitze School of Advanced International Studies (SAIS)
Johns Hopkins University
House Committee on Foreign Affairs
Hearing on "Attacking Hizballah's Financial Network: Policy Options"
June 8, 2017

Chairman Royce, Ranking Member Engel, and Members of the House Committee on Foreign Affairs, thank you for this opportunity to appear before you today to discuss Hizballah. The Committee's leadership on Middle East affairs is essential, and I am grateful for the opportunity to share my expertise and assist with your mission.

Having examined Hizballah as a national security policymaker and as a researcher for nearly two decades, I can confidently say that this is a critical time to assess it. While its nefarious activities have been a concern for the United States since its creation, Hizballah is facing unparalleled challenges amidst a dynamic period in the Middle East. Such challenges can offer opportunities to those opposing Hizballah's deadly mandate, but also present indicators and warnings about further regional instability. Effectively tackling the scourge Hizballah presents by minimizing its financing will benefit from grounding in a political-military context. Today I look forward to doing so and to offering suggestions as to how the Committee should consider acting.

<u>Hizballah's History</u>

A coalescence of events throughout the late 1970s and early 1980s, including the Lebanese civil war, nascent activism among the Lebanese Shia community, the disappearance of a major Shia figure (Imam Musa Sadr), multiple Israeli invasions, and Iran's revolution enabled Hizballah's establishment.[1] Iranian military training and financial assistance to Hizballah began early on and the fruits of its investment were clear in the horrific bombings against American installations in Lebanon throughout the early 1980s, most famously the U.S. Embassy and the Marine barracks. As this Committee's Members know well, before the 9/11 attacks, Hizballah was responsible for the loss of more American lives than any other violent non-state actor.

After Lebanon's civil war ended, its military largely disarmed, demobilized, and reintegrated many of the militias, although traces remained.[2] Hizballah was the only one that was not forced to turn in their weapons after Lebanon's long and bloody civil war. If you go to the Lebanese Ministry of Defense, you will see a memorial to this terrible conflict, which is composed of weapons collected from the various violent groups and

---

[1] Literature on the varied elements that enabled Hizballah's emergence includes Augustus Richard Norton, *Hezbollah: A Short History* (Princeton: Princeton University Press, 2007); Ahmad Nizar Hamzeh, *In the Path of Hizbullah* (Syracuse: Syracuse University Press, 2004); Fouad Ajami, *The Vanished Imam: Musa al Sadr and the Shia of Lebanon* (Ithaca: Cornell University Press, 1986); Ze'ev Schiff and Ehud Ya'ari, *Israel's Lebanon War* (New York: Simon & Schuster, 1985).
[2] Elizabeth Picard, *The Demobilization of the Lebanese Militias* (London: Centre for Lebanese Studies, 1990).

melted together. You will not, however, find Hizballah's stockpile in that pile of rusting metal.

In recent decades, Hizballah has received increasingly sophisticated materiel and training, and financial assistance, from Iran and Syria. As former Secretary of Defense Robert Gates underscored, Hizballah possesses "far more rockets and missiles than most governments in the world."[3] Over the years, it effectively redefined its justification for maintaining its armed capability, allowing it to develop into one of the most well-equipped and best-trained non-state forces in the Middle East.

Since early in its creation, Hizballah has been a complex entity, delivering social services, political support, and at least the perception of security to the Lebanese Shia amid an extremely divided Lebanese polity. Note there are few meaningful and viable alternatives for the community it serves in Lebanon. The substantial assistance Hizballah receives from nefarious actors like Iran and Syria enable it to play a singular role in Lebanon as a political, social, and extremely powerful military force. Without this support, it would simply be another militia or political actor among many in Lebanese society.

<u>Hizballah Today: A Diagnosis</u>

To effectively examine Hizballah today, one must consider the impact and implications of the Syrian conflict, which is entering its seventh year. My diagnosis begins with the following argument: Hizballah has both benefited from and suffered because of its lengthy involvement in this imbroglio.

Hizballah's Losses

On the negative side of the ledger, Hizballah faces profound challenges as it loses domestic support, regional popularity, and likely thousands of fighters courtesy of its efforts to bolster the appalling Assad regime.

It's remarkable to compare Hizballah's popularity today to just over a decade ago, when it fought Israel in a 34-day summer war. Hizballah Secretary-General Hassan Nasrallah was one of the most popular leaders in the Middle East after that conflict. I was the Pentagon's Levant Director at the time, and as we organized the largest non-combatant evacuation of Americans in U.S. history, I couldn't help but be frustrated by Nasrallah's growing fame. Yet that luster has long since faded.

Today, support for Hizballah across the region is much shakier as Sunnis from around the Middle East watch Hizballah aid in the death and destruction of Syria and its people. The Gulf Cooperation Council and the Arab League have declared it a terrorist organization, and the Organization of Islamic Countries has condemned it. While they did so for a number of reasons, not least parochial sectarian ones, their actions demonstrate further isolation of Hizballah around the Middle East.

The Lebanese Shia now watch as body bags of its youth return from waging this ghastly war on behalf of Tehran and Damascus. With estimates of 5,000-10,000 Hezbollah members fighting in Syria in support of Bashar Assad's murderous regime, it is hemorrhaging members like never before; indeed, Hizballah has bled more in Syria

---

[3] Dan De Luce, "Gates: Hezbollah Getting Improved Missiles," Defense News, 27 April 2010.

than in fighting Israel—over a much shorter period of time.[4] And the enormity of these casualties is magnified in such a small community.

Hizballah is waging a counterinsurgency to prop up Assad. The American military has learned over the last decade and a half that this type of conflict is extremely difficult and costly, in blood and in treasure. It has lost important commanders, like Mustafa Badreddine, among others. Moreover, this conflict has been going on for seven years and shows little potential for ending any time soon, increasing the opportunity cost Hizballah is paying.

And perhaps most worrisome for Hizballah, its mission is increasingly questionable. The conflict in Syria is being waged on behalf of Iran and Syria, and it promotes Hizballah's needs, not those of the Lebanese Shia. It is distant from Hizballah's historical emphasis on waging war against Israel, to which it can attribute much of its domestic and regional support historically. By enabling the death of half a million Syrians and the displacement of 11 million Syrian refugees, its rhetoric about defending the weak rings hollow.

Notable power shifts are at play because of the Syria conflict. The Syrian regime owes Hizballah its continued existence. Hizballah, meanwhile, has become more of a regional player—it has a substantial presence in at least four different countries around the Middle East—but it is increasingly exerting Iran's mandate to the detriment of its own community.

It's important to underscore that Hizballah's leadership did not really have a choice about whether to join the Syria conflict, even though many of these costs were likely clear to them. Hizballah initially took a number of steps to hide its malign activity in Syria; Hassan Nasrallah finally owned up to it after nearly a year.[5] But without Tehran's support and Syria's geography, he knew Hizballah would no longer be the most capable force in Lebanon. And from Iran's point of view, the entity it has trained, equipped, and built for decades has enabled Tehran to project power around the region, particularly in places of paramount concern, like Iraq and Syria. If Hizballah wanted to continue playing the singular role it holds in Lebanon, it had to go all in on the Syria conflict.

Hizballah has effectively become part and parcel of the Iranian Revolutionary Guards Corps-Quds Force (IRGC-QF). Qassem Soleimani is the decider now of Hizballah's future—not Hassan Nasrallah. Years ago, I wondered how Hizballah would respond to a profoundly escalatory mission by Tehran. I no longer wonder that today. It is now clear that Soleimani says jump and Hizballah asks how high. The evidence of this shift has grown palpable in recent years—if Iran wants Hizballah to assassinate Lebanese politicians, prop up a murderous Syrian dictator, or kill Israelis, Nasrallah's willingness to debate these missions has become immaterial. The conflict in Syria has shifted the power dynamics between them such "that the relationship is now a boss-employee situation rather than a partnership."[6] As one Lebanese political figure explained,

---

[4] Bilal Y. Saab and Nicholas Blanford, "Will Syria be Hezbollah's Proving Ground, or Its Undoing?" *World Politics Review*, 26 July 2016.

[5] Babak Dehghanpisheh "Hezbollah Becomes Wild Card in Syria," *The Washington Post*, 27 September 2012. Anne Barnard, "Hezbollah Commits to an All-Out Fight to Save Assad," *The New York Times*, 25 May 2013.

[6] Hanin Ghaddar, "Hezbollah Losing Its Luster Under Soleimani," *Policywatch 2766*, 22 February 2017.

"Nasrallah is not going to say 'No' to someone who has given him $30 billion over the past 30 years."[7] Simply put, it now appears that Hizballah is willing to do whatever Iran wants, whenever it asks, and regardless of the cost.

Iran is willing to fight to the last Hizballah member in Syria and it appears Hizballah is, too. That is a problem for Hizballah in many ways, but particularly domestically. The Lebanese Shia are more isolated than they have been in a very long time. They are increasingly disillusioned by Hizballah—which raised their community's stature in Lebanon over the last 30 years—but today they are fearful and see few protectors. Their community is facing deep domestic discontent. Many of those now joining Hizballah are doing so more for monetary than ideological reasons, as Hizballah's shift in recruiting methods has illustrated (e.g., multi-year contracts for new fighters headed to Syria).[8] This skews incentives and invariably influences the very nature of the organization, especially if its new recruits are less enamored with Iran's vision. But, one out of every four Lebanese Shia receives a salary from Hizballah and there is little evidence that other state actors can or would effectively fill this void, even as it grows while Hizballah's emphasis on social services thins out compared to military operations.[9] In light of all of these dynamics, the Lebanese Shia desperately need alternative political representation and new opportunities—particularly in the economic sector.

Hizballah's support at home has grown more precarious and its popularity around the region has plummeted as it has bled on behalf of Damascus and Tehran. Hizballah is out on a limb, a particularly fragile place to be in today's Middle East.

Hizballah's Gains

All that said, Hizballah has also benefited from its involvement in the Syrian conflict. Ten years ago, I was most worried about Hizballah's weapons. We saw during the summer 2006 war with Israel how Hizballah's most destructive weapon in the conflict, Kornet anti-tank rockets, came from the Syrian Ministry of Defense, and other sophisticated materiel streamed from Iran, including the C-802 anti-ship cruise missile that damaged the *INS Hanit*.[10]

Now, I'm more concerned with the experience Hizballah has gained from the Syria conflict. To be sure, it has come at a price. Nevertheless, before the Syria conflict, Hizballah was a capable military force good at a limited number of things. Now, as its portfolio has expanded dramatically, it has become a hardened force adept at facilitating Iranian power projection around the Middle East. Over the last six years, it has become an effective expeditionary force. It has learned how to command and control a complicated conflict in collaboration with a number of other actors. It has acquired substantial real-world fighting experience in diverse environments using increasingly sophistical materiel. And as the operating space in Syria becomes crowded and the U.S.

---

[7] Samia Nakhoul, "Special Report: Hezbollah Gambles All in Syria," *Reuters*, 26 September 2013.
[8] Hanin Ghaddar, "Economic Alternatives Could Help Split Shiites from Hezbollah," *Policywatch 2711*, 18 October 2016.
[9] Ibid.
[10] Adrian Blomfield, "Israel Humbled by Arms from Iran," The Daily Telegraph (London), 15 August 2006. Frank Gardner, "Hezbollah Missile Threat Assessed," British Broadcasting Service, 3 August 2006.

military deepens its direct involvement there, we could see inadvertent or deliberate interactions with Hizballah.

These losses and gains should be monitored throughout the Syrian conflict. How this war ends is a matter of paramount importance for Hizballah. Any outcome short of Assad's survival is problematic. Continued fighting, a hardline Sunni regime, a brokered negotiation courtesy of U.S.-Russian rapprochement—all pose different and serious challenges for Hizballah.

<u>Lebanon's Military and Hizballah</u>

I'd now like to turn to Lebanon, Hezbollah's home base. While the situation in Lebanon appears surprisingly quiet, one should not be lured into thinking it is stable or that serious violence will not erupt. Now for a country of a few million—the exact figure hasn't been precise since the 1932 census—brimming with sizable populations of long-term Palestinian refugees and more recent Syrian ones, and 18 or so different confessional groups, it's a miracle Lebanon still exists in any form at all. And that's important to remember: while the Lebanese state has institutions like a military, a judiciary, and a bureaucracy; these entities are extremely fragile. They do little in the way of actual governing, as we have seen time and time again, and are often beholden to non-state forces or external actors.

Remedying the weakness of Lebanese government institutions has been a key focus area for the U.S. government, as this Committee's Members are well aware. After former Prime Minister Rafi Hariri was assassinated more than ten years ago, the U.S. government sought to strengthen Lebanese government institutions, particularly the military, as a foundation to support a sovereign government that fulfills its basic responsibilities to its citizens. This is a long-term endeavor—and an often-unsatisfying one.

Lebanon's Military

Over the last decade, the Lebanese military has become one of the top recipients of U.S. security assistance. And as one of the architects of the U.S. effort to train and equip Lebanon's military, I am continually asked why the U.S. government is working so hard to build the forces. The answer is simple: it is in the U.S. interest for the Lebanese military to fight nefarious actors whenever it is willing, and without U.S. military assistance, its ability to do so is severely constrained.

When I first began visiting Lebanon nearly 15 years ago, there was little sign of the Lebanese military. This was during the Syrian occupation and it was Syrian forces that I often saw out and about, not Lebanese. When the United States began building the Lebanese military after the Lebanese people pushed out Syria's military, the force was large, unwieldy, had a top-heavy and bloated force structure, lacked the most basic equipment, and spent 90% of its resources on personnel.[11]

---

[11] International Institute for Strategic Studies, *The Military Balance 2004–2005* (London: International Institute for Strategic Studies, 2005), 129–30. Aram Nerguizian, *U.S. Military Assistance to Lebanon: A*

Since then, it has deployed throughout much of Lebanese territory and begun taking important, albeit insufficient steps, to counter violent actors. It has deployed thousands of troops around the country, but especially to southern Lebanon since 2006. In 2007, we saw it successfully battle Fatah al-Islam (FAI) in a bloody urban war—despite Hizballah's Secretary-General arguing that any Lebanese military action would cross a red line.[12] U.S. support made this first big conflict a success, as the U.S. military raced more than forty planeloads of assets to Beirut.[13] It was in our interest then for the Lebanese military to counter FAI, just as it is in our interest today for it to counter radical Sunni groups in Lebanon like Nusra Front and ISIL.

But the 2007 fight is also indicative of the types of conflict the Lebanese military will engage in—those that involve largely consensus opponents. In 2007, a Sunni prime minister ordered a military led by a Maronite Christian to counter a Sunni Palestinian group. The Lebanese government and the Lebanese people supported these actions because they were fighting Palestinians. Today, there's a largely similar dynamic vis-à-vis radical Sunni groups like ISIL. But to be clear, there is absolutely no way a similar level of support would be garnered if the Lebanese military had to take on a more domestic opponent.

Lebanon's military is flawed, but it is nationally supported and well respected—in a country with few institutions that can be described as such. A military force is only as capable as its political leadership permits it to be. While Lebanon's military has grown increasingly capable and taken some meaningful steps for internal security, its government does not hold a monopoly on violence. The military is beholden to a fragile government that is easily manipulated by external parties, their proxies, and other non-state actors; nevertheless, any meaningful attempts by the state's military to secure Lebanese territory and confront heinous actors are in U.S. national interest.

Hizballah and the Lebanese Military

I'd like to address head on the dynamic between Hizballah and Lebanon's military. There is no evidence, to my knowledge, that the Lebanese military has given Hizballah any materiel; indeed, it has an impeccable record of maintaining control over its weapons. I did not fully appreciate how thoroughly the military kept track of its materiel until the 2006 Israel-Hizballah war. When the Israel Defense Forces attacked a Lebanese military base, the LAF leadership wasted no time in providing the Defense Department with a list of the serial numbers of every item at the base. It was clear that Lebanon's military did not want its reputation tarnished if nefarious groups captured any of those weapons.

Second, and let me be blunt here—Hizballah doesn't need the Lebanese military's assets. The weapons it receives from Iran via Syria are substantially more sophisticated than any materiel that the United States has given Lebanon's military to date. And as we

---

Net Assessment and Implications for U.S. Policy (Washington, DC: Center for Strategic and International Studies, 2010), 20; 23.

[12] Nada Bakri and Hassan M. Fattah, "18 Dead in Lebanon as Army and Camp Militants Clash," *The New York Times*, 2 June 2007.

[13] Eric Edelman and Mara Karlin, "Fool me Twice: How the United States Lost Lebanon—Again," *World Affairs* (May/June 2011).

have seen over the last few years—with spontaneous explosions erupting around Damascus, likely courtesy of Israel—Hizballah continues trying to improve its stockpiles. The return addresses are Tehran and Damascus— not the Lebanese Ministry of Defense. Hizballah poses the most potent threat to the Lebanese state's internal security. It turned its weapons on the Lebanese people in 2008 and will do so again if there are meaningful efforts to disarm it.

<u>Implications for U.S. Policy: Questions to Consider</u>

Hizballah's future matters because it is inextricably linked to the future of Iran, Syria, Lebanon, and Israel, among others. As the Committee's Members seek to legislate further U.S. action against Hizballah, I would urge you to ask the following questions over the coming months:

1) What's the Administration's strategy for the Levant? Is it focused on ISIL or does it include the Assad regime's demise, also?
2) How are the regimes in Iran, Syria, and Russia adjusting their support for and/or collaboration with Hizballah in Syria?
3) What points of friction exist between these regimes and Hizballah? And can they be exploited? What about between the Lebanese Shia community and Hizballah?
4) Are any meaningful political or economic alternatives to Hizballah emerging among the Lebanese Shia community? If so, how are they displacing Hizballah's power?
5) In what ways is the new Administration regularly and rigorously assessing its program to strengthen the Lebanese military? Are current levels of security and foreign assistance sufficient and effective?
6) How is the U.S. military accounting for the increased potential of U.S.- Hizballah confrontation in and around Syria?
7) What are the indicators and warnings that Hizballah may seek to reignite conflict with Israel?

This Committee is rightly concerned about Hizballah and how to weaken it. As I have outlined today, there are no simple remedies to the problem Hizballah poses. Anything short of a transformation in Iranian regional behavior means it will remain a threat regionally—and beyond—for the future.

Chairman ROYCE. Thank you. If I could just ask a question here on, I guess a striking lesson in life, which is the zeal for the deal which becomes eventually a deal at any cost, how people get caught up on that. In April, it was reported that the Justice and the State Departments in the Obama administration denied or delayed requests from prosecutors and agents to lure some key Iranian fugitives to friendly countries so that they could be arrested for procuring material for Iran's nuclear program. This is something that Dr. David Albright spoke to before this committee, a former U.N. weapons inspector. He testified that out of a misplaced fear of negatively affecting the deal, the Obama administration also interfered in U.S. law enforcement efforts.

So it is with interest to note Dr. Asher's testimony this morning, because in that testimony, he says: "In narrow pursuit of the Iran nuclear agreement, the administration actively mitigated investigations and prosecutions needed to effectively dismantle Hezbollah in the Iran action network. Senior leadership presiding, directing, and overseeing various sections within the Department of Justice, the Department of Homeland Security, the Department of State, and portions of the U.S. intelligence community, systematically disbanded any action that threatened to derail the administration's policy agenda focused on Iran."

So I was going to ask Dr. Asher what details you could give us on that and maybe ask Mr. Maltz your opinion as well. Dr. Asher?

Mr. ASHER. Well, I had the unfortunate experience of being at the State Department coming back to work on the counter ISIL economic warfare plan as the coordinating under General Allen, so I saw a lot of this happening. This was after I departed the Hezbollah effort, largely because it was being defunded inside the DOD. And so I saw a lot of this directly, you know, we had money flowing, pallets and pallets of money flowing to Iran. There was a lot of stuff. Let's recall, in fairness, the Bush administration stripped the Department of Justice of its authorities to indict the Government of North Korea, to pursue the North Korean nuclear program, which we had a very sophisticated plan to destroy.

Chairman ROYCE. Another case of the zeal for the deal.

Mr. ASHER. Another case of the zeal for the deal. I predicted to my colleagues that by the end of the Obama administration, we would see the same dynamics. This is a bipartisan syndrome, okay? It is not, you know, blame the Obama administration, blame the Bush administration. There is something about people wanting to have a deal at almost any cost. And in the case of the Iran deal, there are a lot of things around here talking about the nuclear negotiations, but there is no provision, as we discussed before, in outsourcing, even though they built a North Korea nuclear reactor in Syria right under the noses, right under the Six Party talk. There are a lot of holes in this cheese. Law enforcement didn't have to be one of them. It doesn't have to be one of them. People respect, including in Iran and Lebanon, when laws are enforced. The arrest recently of Kassim Tajideen, one of the most important super facilitators for Iran and Hezbollah, has sent a shock wave through the leadership of Hezbollah and the Iranian regime. The fact that we have him in prison here and that maybe he might cooperate, I am sure that has gotten their attention.

We had the ability, I can't comment on those two operations which I am aware of, that were essentially aborted, but we had many more that we were inhibited from acting on, for political reasons. We had operations that were denied overseas; we had funding that was cut. People were making a decision that the counterterrorism mission and the Iran nuclear deal was a central and all-important element, whereas containing Iran's malevolent forces was less important. I think you can do both, and we have to do both. I don't think it is an either/or.

If the Iranians don't like it, too bad, they blew up our Embassy twice, they killed hundreds of Marines. They went after us in Iraq when I was working with the Special Operations Task Force in support of them there, and killed nearly 800 Americans with explosively formed projectiles designed by Hezbollah. I have a beef against these people, obviously. And we have the tools, thanks to the great work of the DEA and other law enforcement agencies, to take them apart financially, economically, politically, and strategically, using law enforcement which the world will respect.

Chairman ROYCE. And maybe also I will ask Mr. Maltz what steps do we need to take? What steps does Congress need to take to rebuild our enforcement capabilities there?

Mr. MALTZ. Well, like I said, sir, the Special Operations division has a history of success. As a matter of fact, you were very, very supportive in the Viktor Bout case. The last time I was before you was when you supported the DEA on the extradition of Viktor Bout, so I will never forget that. Thank you.

Chairman ROYCE. By the way it sends a powerful message to a lot of other miscreants on this globe, the fact that he is behind bars, and thank you very much for your success on that.

Mr. MALTZ. So on that note, SOD had had this counter narco-terrorism operation center for the purpose of coordinating these type of investigations. We created that to provide a unity of effort. That is the purpose, because we are in this together. You cannot separate out the terrorist aspects and the criminal aspects, because at the end of the day, it is what is in the best interest of the U.S. Government. So I compliment some folks in the government in the Department of Justice and Admiral McRaven specifically, because we organized a U.S. Government interagency effort on this threat. And every agency that came to the table agreed that Hezbollah was a priority against the United States. So the idea was to put all the resources on the table. We went down to Florida for this big government meeting where the Attorney General, the Department of Homeland Security Director, and all these other officials were there.

So the idea would be, let's put the stuff on the table and work together. As soon as we left the meeting and as soon as Admiral McRaven retired, it fell apart, in my view. And I was the one in charge of the operation at SOD, so I could say that very clearly. And so for me, how the heck can you have an action against this organization running the Southern District of New York, the best in the country, and interagency did not come together and provide the necessary information to make it a more powerful action. So we had the right concept, but we didn't complete the deal. You know how upset I was when I saw The Wall Street Journal article at the end of last year? Very much—very accurate article. The car parks are booming in west Africa because the business is booming. We had a chance to knock them dead, and we held back because of interagency cooperation. So we have to end it.

Chairman ROYCE. We are going to return to that issue. I have to go to Mr. Deutch, and thank you.

Mr. DEUTCH. Thank you, Mr. Chairman. And thank you to the witnesses for a really excellent presentation.

Dr. Karlin, you said that Qassem Soleimani is now the decider of Hezbollah's future, and you talked about using Hezbollah for Iranian power projection. My question is how that is done, and whether it is Iraq, or Yemen, Bahrain, UAE, Saudis, are you suggesting that Hezbollah, or can you speak to whether Hezbollah is more than a model for the terrorist groups looking to act in those countries, and is, in fact, playing an operational role. If so, how broadly?

Ms. KARLIN. Thank you for that question, Mr. Deutch. Hezbollah is the best design model Iran could have really hoped for in a number of ways. And I think when you look at attempts to build a similar force, say, Iranian support to the Houthis, it is just not going to be equivalent for domestic Yemeni reasons, among others. But, I think, for those of us who spent so long looking at Hezbollah, it was always a question of, if Iran asked Hezbollah to get involved in circumstances that would be really problematic domestically, what would Hezbollah do?

This was particularly thought of if there was some sort of entanglement between Israel and Iran, what would Hezbollah do if this ended up being a problem? And what we have seen is because Hezbollah can only play its singular role in Lebanon with Iran's weapons, what is happening now is existential for it.

And so this debate that used to occur doesn't occur anymore. Indeed, any thoughts Nasrallah might have are immaterial. If someone like Qassem Soleimani needs Hezbollah to go bleed in Syria, he doesn't really have a choice anymore, which is why you see not just the bleeding in Syria, which is obviously really problematic from a domestic and regional support perspective, but Hezbollah getting involved in training Houthis in Yemen, also not core to its interests really at all.

It doesn't have a whole lot of options here. And we have seen this ability so that when we put on, say, U.S. Defense Department hats, one worries about Iran's conventional military, but it is the ability to build these violent nonstate actors like Hezbollah, and then deploy them in the various circumstances against their own interests in really problematic and lethal ways.

Mr. DEUTCH. I appreciate that. Dr. Levitt, in 2012, a bipartisan group of members began sending letters to our EU partners, urging them to designate Hezbollah. In 2013, they declared Hezbollah's military wing a terrorist organization. And as I mentioned earlier in my comments, the U.S. and others don't make this distinction between political and military wings. What impact would a full designation from the EU have on Hezbollah's ability to operate on the continent? And what more could the U.S. be doing now to encourage the EU to declare Hezbollah, in its entirety, a terrorist organization?

Mr. LEVITT. Thank you for the question. When this was going on, my book on Hezbollah had just been finished and spent 8 months with Georgetown University press, God bless them, till it came out. That gave me an opportunity to make seven, eight, nine different trips to Europe, Brussels and most capitals at the time trying to push them on this issue.

Some of their concerns were some of the concerns you heard earlier about reprisals, about who are we to ban an entity that is duly elected in Lebanon? For many of the governments, however, at the end of day, their decision to ban even part of Hezbollah, the military and terrorist wing, had nothing to do with what terrorism Hezbollah had carried out around the world, let alone in Europe, but had everything to do with Syria. And so, that provided us a real opportunity.

What the legislation in Europe does already is it gives us an opportunity to go to the Europeans and get them to cooperate with us on Hezbollah investigations related to the terrorism and military activities, but Hezbollah is a large movement, and it doesn't operate a Hezbollah terrorism incorporated. And so it is often very difficult to explain to the Europeans, or prove to the Europeans, in open source, in a way that they can go public with, that an entity we want to target with them is, in fact, related to the military and terrorist wing, and not just politics or social welfare. Banning all of Hezbollah would end that debate and discussion, and it would stop giving Hezbollah a pass in which it could just, through basic front organizations and money laundering, pretend that something is a legitimate actor, part of their "legitimate side of the house," when, in fact, it is supporting, or also supporting the terrorist and military activities.

If I may follow up also on the earlier question related to this. I don't think we can just target Hezbollah anymore. We need to bring this into a larger picture in targeting the Iran threat or the Iran action network more broadly. In particular, the Shia militias that are now so active in Iraq and in Syria. I think the likelihood that we could see some direct conflict between U.S. forces and these, including Hezbollah in Tanf from southern Syria is very, very real. And what we need to realize is that many of these Shia militants are not going to go back to being pharmacists and farmers when the immediate conflict is over in Iraq or in Syria.

And that means that we are seeing, right now, right before our eyes, the creation of an Iranian foreign legion of people who can go and do things for them in an asymmetric kind of way that Mara was talking about. It reminds me of Hezbollah and Iran's proxies just a few years after the Iranian revolution, where Iran wanted attacks carried out against U.S. and other interests, say, for example, in Kuwait. And they sent Hezbollah operatives and they sent Iraqi Shia operatives. Some of the same people operating today, people like Hadeel Ammari, people like Abu Mahdi al-Muhandis, the very same people, these relationships go back 30 years. And we need to be targeting of course Hezbollah but not only Hezbollah. The Europeans as well.

Chairman ROYCE. We will go to Ileana Ros-Lehtinen.

Ms. ROS-LEHTINEN. Thank you so much, Mr. Chairman and the ranking member.

Hezbollah is one of the most dangerous and formidable terror organizations in the world responsible for some of history's most notorious terror attacks. As Dr. Karlin noted, Hezbollah is more than just a partner in the Iranian regime, it is an extension of Iran's IRGC Quds Force and it is fulfilling Tehran's every wish, including propping up the murderous Assad regime in Syria, a mission which has only increased Hezbollah's sophistication, its stockpile, and its capabilities. We cannot ignore Hezbollah's influence and control over the Lebanese state, and by extension, the Lebanese Armed Forces, or LAF.

In your written testimony, Dr. Karlin, you state that the LAF is "easily manipulated" and "only as capable as its political leadership permits." So if the LAF is easily manipulated, and Hezbollah has such a large influence over Lebanese institutions, how can we, in the U.S., reconcile U.S. support for the LAF? And I would like to hear the other witnesses respond to that, also.

And even with some of the safeguards that are in place, are we not running the risk of U.S. assistance to the LAF indirectly helping Hezbollah?

Ms. KARLIN. Thank you for that question. If I might start with a little bit of history, the very first time I went to Lebanon was during the Syrian occupation——

Ms. ROS-LEHTINEN. Well, thank you, Dr. Karlin. I do appreciate history, but I only have 3 minutes. How can we reconcile? How can both things be true? It is, LAF is "easily manipulated, it is only as capable as the political leadership permits" and yet we support the LAF. It is confusing, yes?

Ms. KARLIN. Ideally, we want the Lebanese Government to be able to secure its territory, right, to have a monopoly on violence. And the more that there are violent nonstate actors that exist and proliferate around Lebanon, whether it is groups like Hezbollah, or it is groups within the refugee camps, like we have seen with Fatah Islam historically, the more that we want the Lebanese military to be capable of trying to shrink that operating space.

Ms. ROS-LEHTINEN. Thank you. And how about the other witnesses, if you care to comment?

Mr. LEVITT. The other witnesses are all pointing to me. I would just say that you are absolutely right, it is complicated. The LAF has done some very good things in taking the fight to the Islamic State, for example, but the LAF is compromised, even as it is the most basic glue that holds the Lebanese state together. So I think what we need to do is try and have as much influence with the LAF as possible, and understand that our expectations need to be limited, and that explains why, sometimes, we are very careful with what weapon systems we provide.

Ms. ROS-LEHTINEN. Thank you. Let me just get to one last question. The U.S. Government has issued an interagency report stating that there are links, as we have discussed, between cigarette smuggling and terrorist organizations, such as Hezbollah. Do you have any recommendations on what we can do in Congress or the administration should do to clamp down on this source of funding for Hezbollah and other terrorist groups?

Mr. ASHER. I mean, there is no doubt that we saw, in many cases, the cigarettes being moved away, same route, same facilitation networks as the cocaine. So one of the best ways to do this is a public-private partnership. I had a great opportunity when I was running the North Korea illicit activities initiative and actually partnered with the Secret Service and the Philip Morris Corporation. It actually worked. We let the people affected by the cigarettes underwrite some of the law enforcement activities and we got support from members.

Ms. ROS-LEHTINEN. So you would recommend——

Mr. ASHER. I think we can do a lot together with the private sector to go after this, but we need to have a joint task force. This is the most important element, because these are polymorphic crimes. It is not just cocaine smuggling or Captagon. They are basically doing anything they can make a buck on, and cigarette smuggling is definitely one of them.

Ms. ROS-LEHTINEN. Thank you.

Any other comments?

Mr. MALTZ. I would say that, in my experience, one of the last cases that I was involved with at the SOD was another very disturbing trend, groups from Yemen operating all over the United States, involved with cigarette, unpacked cigarettes, K2 and spice, EBT fraud counterfeit goods and sending millions and millions of dollars right back to Yemen. So we have these global trade-based schemes going on from America back to these countries. So we have to step up the efforts.

Ms. ROS-LEHTINEN. Thank you so much. Mr. Schneider?

Chairman ROYCE. I think Mr. Brad Schneider is next.

Mr. SCHNEIDER. Thank you. And I, again, want to thank the committee for calling this hearing, the witnesses for your testimony, but also for your long and dedicated work on this issue. We talked, in this hearing, quite a bit about the link between Iran and Hezbollah, Hezbollah's international activity, and the impact of Syria. Dr. Karlin, I think you said it very well, what I would look for, and I am anxious to understand better, is the administration's strategy for the Levant and how we take that on. I only have 5 minutes, so I am going to say I want to see it and we can talk about it later.

I would like to bring an issue that we haven't talked about here, and that is Russia's involvement with Hezbollah. To what extent— maybe I will turn it to you, Dr. Karlin—to what extent have you seen Russian cooperation with Hezbollah and Syria?

Ms. KARLIN. Thank you. At a tactical and operational level we have seen Russian air cover for Hezbollah ground movement, we have seen the likelihood of joint operating centers, that is worrisome. What worries me a lot more is that Russia's military, if you follow its modernization over the years, has gotten pretty good. And I worry about Hezbollah learning about things, like how to use cyber warfare, how to use electronic warfare. It is worth noting, however, that strategically, this is a relationship of convenience. This conflict is existential for Hezbollah and Syria, it is not for the Russians.

Mr. SCHNEIDER. But I know it was reported last year in the Daily Beast, I believe, that Russia was providing Hezbollah long-range tactical missiles and other material. Have you seen that, and is there any evidence that the relationship is going to outlast the Syrian conflict?

Ms. KARLIN. I have not seen evidence of that beyond those reports which I have also read. Russia has its own problems with groups like Hezbollah, which is why I still see this as a relationship of convenience rather than an actual partnership or alliance. And indeed, it is conceivable that the Russians will want to come to a serious negotiation on Syria way before Hezbollah will, because it is just not in their interest for a Syrian conflict to turn out any other way than Assad remaining in power.

Mr. SCHNEIDER. Great, thank you. I am going to turn to Dr. Levitt in a little different direction. You talked a fair amount about the Hezbollah International Financing Prevention Act. Thank you for your help with that. A broader question—what metric should we be using to determine whether or not it is working, and what steps we should take further to push forward?

Mr. LEVITT. First of all, let me thank you for your leadership on the Hezbollah International Financial Prevention Act. You were involved in this in the very, very beginning before many others were. I think there are so many tools here, that we were using some of them as you heard, and then we all but stopped. And in order to have a real effect, you have to have some continuity. There were prosecutions that were put on ice. There were designations that didn't happen. The fact that Kassim Tajideen was—we worked with the Moroccans, he was arrested in Morocco, he was extradited to the United States. He is now here in Washington, DC, in custody, been indicted. That I think is a very, very, positive sign, but there is a lot more that has to happen, across the interagency. The type of interagency cooperation that we have had in the past and we now need to have looking forward that you heard from myself and from my colleagues.

I also think we lost a real opportunity under the original HIFPA, the decision on whether or not to designate Hezbollah as a transnational organized criminal enterprise was given not to law enforcement, but to the DNI. And that decision was largely politicized and didn't move forward. It really boggled the mind. I wrote about it at the time. There may be reasons to decide not to move forward with it that I would disagree with, but there is no question that Hezbollah operates as a transnational organized criminal enterprise, and to designate them as such would really not only tar and feather them, but give us even more opportunities to target them.

Again, I think that Mara Karlin is right, that Qassem Soleimani is calling the shots more than anybody else. And the reason for that is because Hezbollah is so incredibly beholden to Iran for funds and weapons, and its position, which means that we need to be targeting not only Hezbollah operatives, but also the Iranian operatives and entities that are overseeing this relationship, which means getting comfortable with the idea of holding Iran's feet to the fire for its support for terrorism in particular, leaving the human rights and ballistic missiles aside, which we should be doing as well in the context of the Iran deal. This does not undermine or cross the Iran deal.

Mr. SCHNEIDER. Thank you. I am almost out of time. So let me just reiterate: I agree with you. I think we have to hold Iran to account for its activities, not just support of terrorism throughout the world, but also its activities within the region and its human rights activities at home. And I agree with what you said earlier; I don't think that threatens the JCPOA.

So, again, thank you to the witnesses,

And, with that, I yield back.

Chairman ROYCE. We go to Mr. Dan Rohrabacher of California.

Mr. ROHRABACHER. Thank you very much, Mr. Chairman, and thank you for your leadership on, again, another really important issue for the safety of our country.

Let me ask some fundamental questions. Is Hezbollah, the people who make up Hezbollah, are they all Palestinians?

Mr. ASHER. No.

Mr. ROHRABACHER. Tell me what Hezbollah is made up of then.

Mr. LEVITT. Hezbollah is a Lebanese group. It is not a Palestinian group——

Mr. ROHRABACHER. Okay. But——

Mr. LEVITT [continuing]. Comprised primarily of Lebanese Shiites.

Mr. ROHRABACHER. I guess the reason I was asking that is that we know that large numbers of Palestinians went to Lebanon, and I assumed that that was the group that eventually became Hezbollah. That is not correct?

Mr. LEVITT. No. When it was founded, it got support from Fatah and other Palestinian groups to be sure and Imad Mughniyah and others. It does also see other sub-units. There is a Sunni sub-unit that includes some Palestinians called the Resistance Brigades, but that is not Hezbollah.

Mr. ROHRABACHER. So they are Lebanese?

Mr. LEVITT. Yes.

Mr. ASHER. Mr. Rohrabacher, I can assure you that Imad Mughniyah himself studied at the financial feet of Yasser Arafat, and it is an interesting—and operationally and financially, we have a very substantial relationship between Palestinian Islamic jihad financiers and Hezbollah's Islamic jihad organization, i.e., the terrorist wing.

So it is a very interesting question, and they are based around a place called Burj al-Barajneh, which is near the airport. That was the historical base of the Palestinian Islamist jihad. It is interesting that there is so much of the Hezbollah terrorist and military wing activity right there, as well.

Ms. KARLIN. Sir, if I might add, I have been to Burj al-Barajneh, and it is worth noting that actually traditionally the relationship between Hezbollah and the Palestinians in Lebanon is quite fraught because the Palestinians in Lebanon are Sunni. Hezbollah is Shia. And when the Palestinian refugees came to Lebanon, they threw off a very delicate confessional balance. So it is a very complicated thing, sir.

Mr. ROHRABACHER. Yes, it is very complicated, and that is the reason why I asked that question. I have always been under the assumption that, yes, they were from Lebanon, but they were basically Palestinian refugees that are now Lebanese. So thank you for clarifying that.

What is the budget for Hezbollah? Do we have an overall budget? Anybody?

Mr. LEVITT. No.

Mr. ROHRABACHER. No?

Mr. LEVITT. Hundreds of millions at a minimum, but I have seen no open-source and—I mean, no open-source numbers——

Mr. ROHRABACHER [continuing]. Do they put those hundreds of millions in a bank somewhere?

Mr. LEVITT. Pardon?

Mr. ROHRABACHER. Do they put those hundreds of millions in a bank? Do they have bank accounts, because I thought this is what this was all about today.

Mr. LEVITT. So, when we got inside the Lebanese Canadian Bank, which we did one way or another, we observed billions of dollars that were under the control both of the Lebanese Hezbollah, which we knew which accounts they were and how much money was in them through unclassified means, as well as Iranian money, and it was billions of dollars, too.

Mr. ROHRABACHER. What banks were those again?

Mr. ASHER. The Lebanese Canadian Bank, but there were many others that were part of a network. Everything we saw was larger than anyone expected.

And the other thing was that the connection to money laundering and drug trafficking proceeds were much greater than we ever expected.

Mr. ROHRABACHER. Okay. So, if we know they have billions of dollars or hundreds of millions of dollars in these banks, can't we do something about that? Aren't we just—if nothing else, I mean, we could use our ability to hack into systems and destroy their bank accounts.

Mr. MALTZ. Sir, like I said before, we did identify $150 million sitting in a bank, Banque Libano-Francaise, and we did—because of the great work in the U.S. with the Southern District of New York—seize $150 million. They transferred the money to the U.S. Marshals' account from Lebanon, and we forfeited $102 million.

Mr. ROHRABACHER. Congratulations on that.

Mr. MALTZ. But there is a lot more.

Mr. ROHRABACHER. Why aren't we doing more of it then? They are still there.

Mr. MALTZ. Well, if we get the interagency task force together and we enforce some accountability on the folks involved, then we can do a lot more.

Mr. ROHRABACHER. Okay.

I have just a couple more seconds here. Let me just note that we have recently seen an attack on Iran and the Iranian Government. The mullahs believe the Sunni forces have attacked them. This may signal a ratcheting up of certain commitments by the United States of America. And as far as I am concerned—I just want to make this point and see what you think—isn't it a good thing for us to have the United States finally backing up Sunnis who will attack Hezbollah and the Shiite threat to us? Isn't that a good thing? And if so, maybe it is a Trump strategy of actually supporting one group against another, considering that you have two terrorist organizations.

Mr. LEVITT. Those attacks were claimed by the Islamic State. It is never in our interest to support a terrorist group like the Islamic State. We should condemn the attacks in Iran, as——

Mr. ROHRABACHER. Even——

Mr. LEVITT [continuing]. We should condemn any act of terrorism, even as we hold Iran accountable for its sponsorship of terrorism.

Mr. ROHRABACHER. So that is like Joe Stalin was a horrible guy; we must never associate with horrible guys like that, even to get Hitler. And so maybe it is a good idea to have radical Muslim terrorists fighting each other. I will leave it at that. Thank you.

Mr. ASHER. I mean, having coordinated the economic warfare plan against the Islamic State, I would not condone an attack by the Islamic State, much like Matt. I would be determined to destroy them financially——

Mr. ROHRABACHER [continuing]. Hezbollah——

Chairman ROYCE. I think we need to go to Joaquin Castro here from Texas for his time.

Mr. CASTRO. Thank you, Chairman.

And thank you, the witnesses, for being here today and for your testimony.

Dr. Karlin, I wanted to follow up on a point that you were making or ask a question based on a point that you made. We know that Russia has assisted and helped Hezbollah. And, of course, we have been dealing in our Nation with the prowess of Russia's cyber capabilities and their abilities for cyber malfeasance.

Can you talk about your concern, if you have a concern, that they are sharing this information or this ability, capabilities, with groups like Hezbollah, and do we have an assessment of what Hezbollah's cyber capabilities are right now and terrorists groups like them?

Ms. KARLIN. Thank you for that question. I have not seen an unclassified assessment of Hezbollah's cyber capabilities.

What I might say on the Russian military front, and my most recent job as the Deputy Assistant Secretary for Strategy and Force Development meant I spend a lot of time thinking about Russian military modernization and the trajectory that it is on, and it is pretty worrisome because not only do we see Russian investments in kind of weapons like its nuclear stockpile, but we also see some worrisome doctrine.

So the Russians have what is known as the Gerasimov Doctrine: Escalate to deescalate. The idea is that if I punch you, you should punch me a whole lot harder so that I give up. That is a pretty dangerous doctrine to play around with, and I worry about Hezbollah not necessarily getting the weapons from Russia, but I worry about them watching how Russia uses its doctrine, employs its doctrine, and then maybe starting to use it itself, say, vis—vis Israel.

Mr. CASTRO. But certainly they could be trained in some of these essential capabilities?

Ms. KARLIN. Oh, absolutely conceivable.

Mr. CASTRO. Sure. And then it is interesting: Obviously, we consider Hezbollah a terrorist organization, but they also have some measure of political control in municipal governments in Lebanon, Parliament seats, which makes them almost a hybrid of a state actor and a nonstate actor, you know, versus ISIS, right, which doesn't seek to elect people, at least as far as we can tell, in the same way in politics.

So let me ask you guys, what do you see them as? Do you see them as a state actor or as a nonstate actor? I open that up to the panel.

Mr. LEVITT. Thanks for the question. You are right: They are both. But we need to see them as a nonstate actor in terms of the explicitly illicit conduct that they are conducting around the world as a transnational criminal organization, as a terrorist organization, and as a militia independent of Lebanon.

They are able to do that function even as they run for municipal government and they run for Parliament and they hold ministerial positions, because we allow it. If you allow an organization that, independent of the country, does all these other things, then, also, by the way, has people run for office, then it can pretend to have more legitimacy than it does.

But I think Mara Karlin was right: The greatest threat to Lebanon, on so many levels—financial, stability—is Hezbollah. And I think it is in part our fault, the international community's fault, as Mr. Deutch suggested, for failing to see Hezbollah holistically as a group that, whatever else it is involved in, it is very much involved in a whole host of explicitly illicit activities, as Mara pointed out, that have nothing to do with the interests of Lebanon, even its interests as a party in Lebanon.

So, ultimately, it is a nonstate actor that engages in some state activities because it benefits them to do so.

Ms. KARLIN. Mr. Castro, I couldn't agree more with Matt's comments. I might just add that the weaker the Lebanese state is, the better it is for Hezbollah.

Mr. ASHER. Just if I could add, we identified publicly in DEA the business affairs component of the Islamist jihad terrorist wing of Hezbollah, the military wing of Hezbollah, as at the center of the narcotrafficking, money laundering conspiracy that involved the Lebanese Canadian Bank, a massive number of cells in Europe distributing cocaine, cocaine coming into the United States. So there is no doubt—and I am not trying to say we shouldn't go after the entire organization, designate the entire organization—but the case that could be made most directly from a law enforcement perspective just following the facts would tie the terrorist wing under Imad Mughniyah, who died, and his successor and his business manager Adham Tabaja, who he designated, to the cocaine money laundering.

So there is a strategy that could be pursued where we go after the business affairs component of Islamist jihad, charge Islamist jihad for having blown up our Embassies and killed our people, and we leave the rest of Hezbollah sort of off to the side. That is an option that some prosecutors have advocated, but I am not sure that that is necessarily really comporting with the facts fully.

Mr. LEVITT. I will just add to that. This is where people get most uncomfortable, right? If you really dig down to the information, you will find time and again that the "political" or "social welfare leadership" is involved in all of this illicit activity. The business affairs component was directly tied to Abdallah Safieddine. Safieddine is a political senior Hezbollah official.

And so, for those who are uncomfortable recognizing that Hezbollah actually is one holistic entity, for those who are uncomfortable with the consequences of having to follow the evidence to where it leads, that may explain why some people are hesitant to do so. It is inexcusable. We should be following the evidence where it takes us, whether it is in a murder case or a bank robbery case or a terrorism case.

Mr. CASTRO. Thank you.

I yield back, Mr. Chairman.

Chairman ROYCE. Mr. Perry.

Mr. PERRY. Thanks, Mr. Chairman.

Thanks to the panel.

Generally speaking, maybe it is Dr. Levitt and Dr. Asher, why shouldn't the U.S. Treasury Department sanction the Central Bank of Lebanon?

Mr. LEVITT. The simple answer is because they are actually very good partners. The Central Bank of Lebanon put out a circular making sure that the Lebanese financial system would enforce things like HIFPA and did a very good job of doing so.

As Mara said before, completely destabilizing Lebanon, destabilizing the financial system there is not in our interest, and of the partners we have, they are one of the best.

Mr. PERRY. Are they facilitating payments that benefit Hezbollah?

Mr. LEVITT. I can't answer that question in any specificity. Because Hezbollah has such a large footprint in the Lebanese economy, it is likely that that happens at some point. Would you, by targeting the Lebanese Central Bank, at the end of the day have a net benefit? No.

Mr. PERRY. Okay. Why shouldn't the Department sanction Iranian banks for which sanctions were lifted under the JCPOA? Anybody?

Mr. LEVITT. My colleagues keep looking at me. That is fine.

I think that we need to be careful that banks that were delisted, when we look at them for relisting or we look at other banks, we are very, very careful and specific to make sure that we are doing these under the authorities that still exist, and they do exist. There will be people who will tell you that you can't redesignate an Iranian entity that was taken off the list, but if it was taken off a proliferation list and it is still today involved, for example, in sponsorship of terrorism, it absolutely can and should be——

Mr. PERRY. And should be, right?

Mr. LEVITT [continuing]. Considered for designation.

Mr. PERRY. Okay.

Mr. ASHER. We are legally mandated, essentially, to do this. That is something, from your oversight perspective, Mr. Perry, that you can remind people. We have a legal responsibility to enforce this act, and we can't willfully ignore the facts. I, unfortunately, have seen a lot of willful ignorance in my career as——

Mr. PERRY. You can't use the JCPOA to be derelict in your duty, right?

Mr. ASHER. That is right.

Mr. PERRY. And that is what is happening in this case——

Mr. ASHER. And it is happening.

Mr. PERRY. Considering they are intensifying international criminal activities, is there any reason the administration shouldn't consider designating Hezbollah as a transnational criminal organization?

Mr. LEVITT. They absolutely should. As I said in my testimony and get into more detail in the written testimony, we should revisit this immediately.

Mr. PERRY. Is there any disagreement among the panel?

Some of the most lucrative activities happen in the TBA, the Tri-Border Area. Can any of you talk about the current measures and what additional measures should be included regarding their criminal syndicate activities in Latin America, et cetera? Anybody?

Mr. MALTZ. All I can say, sir, is that, when I was the head of the SOD, we saw a lot of cocaine leaving the TBA, going all over to the world, working closely with folks in Venezuela, connected to the highest levels of the government in Venezuela, but as far as currently, I can't give you an accurate assessment of what they are seeing in the TBA now.

Mr. PERRY. And what is your recommendation for continued or further action in that regard?

Mr. MALTZ. Again, like I have said all along, the best recommendation I can give to this committee: It has to start with information sharing. Let's stop pushing it under the rug. Get the experts together in a room, designate these as priorities. Every agency should be mandated to put the information on the table and then focus on the targets, and that is not happening.

Mr. ASHER. If I could just say, I think the most powerful current way for the Department of Justice to impose a huge legal penalty against Lebanese Hezbollah, including its terrorist wing, would be to actively prosecute the government of Nicolas Maduro and his associates, including Tareck El Aissami, his executive vice president, for their involvement and complicity and active conduct in cooperating with Hezbollah in narcotrafficking money laundering on an international scale.

Mr. PERRY. Okay.

Mr. LEVITT. If I can add one last thing here.

Mr. PERRY. Sure.

Mr. LEVITT. Again, under HIFPA, we can apply secondary sanctions—and as I described in my testimony at length, so I won't describe it now—we can and should be looking for secondary sanctions, financial institutions with which we can hit secondary sanctions, in particular in South America and, after the Waked Money Laundering Organization was shut down, we saw a lot of that movement interest the Tri-Border Area, Paraguay in particular. There are no shortage of targets.

Mr. PERRY. Okay.

Dr. Asher, Dr. Levitt, and Mr. Maltz, and I guess Dr. Karlin, as well, I did some time in Iraq. I just want, if you can in the few moments that are remaining, to assess the role of Iraqi financial institutions and businesses in enabling Hezbollah in Iran.

Mr. LEVITT. We do know that, in the wake of the original HIFPA legislation, some Hezbollah money was moved out of Lebanon for fear that it wasn't quite as safe there as it once might have been, and some of it was moved, we understand, to places like Dubai and to Iraq.

The first order of business is to try and pressure the Iraqi Government to work as closely with us as possible in ways that they already have, for example, on countering the Islamic State financing, exchange houses, et cetera. Then, short of that, if there are illicit banks that are still providing these types of services knowingly, then we should consider the secondary sanctions option. But that doesn't need to be our first choice. But we definitely need to be working further on the financial system as it relates to these threats.

Mr. ASHER. Very quickly, based on open-source commercial records, you can see a very significant movement of Hezbollah financial operatives tied to the business affairs component of Islamist jihad into Iraq in the last few years. They have established a whole string of businesses in the south in partnership with Iraqi militant groups. It is obviously part of some sort of strategy that they are executing for their Iranian friends.

Mr. PERRY. Just for clarification, in the south, do you mean in places like Basra and Nasiriyah?

Mr. ASHER. Yes, but also into the southern belts of Baghdad as well, so you see it in some of the mixed areas. They have an economic action plan that they are executing to infiltrate the Iraqi economy, with the Lebanese playing a much more significant role.

Chairman ROYCE. We go now to Dan Donovan from New York.

Mr. DONOVAN. Thank you, Mr. Chairman.

Dr. Levitt, during your testimony, you talked about how we should again sanction Iran. Last year, the United States Government paid Iran $1.7 billion to their government. The official purpose of that was a payment for $400 million for a contract for military weapons from decades ago. The remaining $1.3 billion was the interest that was collected on that $400 million while it remained in the United States. If we are going to sanction countries, if we are going to sanction entities, what kind of message do we send them when they are receiving a benefit for us freezing their assets in the United States, that $1.3 billion that they gained in interest?

Mr. LEVITT. So that action was, I believe, an unfortunate but a technical action in terms of the interest. Interest was there. Whether that had to be done or not is another discussion for another time. My feeling is we are where we are. That happened. There is no undoing that. And what we need to do, I believe in keeping with the Iran deal, whether you like the Iran deal or not, whether I like the Iran deal or not, is to hold Iran's feet to the fire on its continuing illicit conduct because that was how the deal was sold to us.

We were told by the previous administration's officials time and again that we would continue to hold their feet to the fire on these issues. We need to. It does not violate the deal to do so. The problem is, because we didn't do anything, Iran has been emboldened. Because we didn't do anything and Iran went around the world, including the Governor of the Central Bank who came here and spoke in Washington, DC, at the Council on Foreign Relations and elsewhere and said the era of sanctions is over, people started buying that narrative. That narrative is false. And so the first thing we need to do is push back on that narrative with our European and Asian allies, make them understand—I hope, because we are where we are—that we will hold up to the letter of the Iran deal, which means enforcing terrorism, ballistic missile, and human rights sanctions.

Mr. ASHER. So I have on my cell phone some pictures that were sent to me by a financial source who is not a U.S. Government source. I do some work for financial institutions on anti-money laundering sanctions compliance, and that source sent me pictures of $1 billion in two pallets of shrink-wrapped U.S. Federal Reserve $100 bill notes that were moved through a European country into West Africa and into a South American country by Iranian agents, it appears, to set up some sort of port-to-port scheme, perhaps involving narcotics trafficking. Whether the money is the money that was given by my State Department colleagues, unfortunately, in my mind, or not—you don't see $1 billion in palletized cash with Federal Reserve Bank of New York symbols on them, the wrappers, every day—the fact is that money is being moved around for operational and devious reasons. I don't think it contributed whatsoever to creating a more peaceful relationship with the Iranian people.

Mr. DONOVAN. You know, I always ask witnesses when they testify before us that we are lawmakers, and, you know, we create laws, and we have to ask experts like you, what laws would you like to see Congress create that would achieve the goals that we all have here?

Would each of you be able to just tell me for a moment what you would think about a law that would prohibit a terrorist organization or a state terrorist organization from receiving a benefit from having their assets in a United States bank?

Mr. ASHER. I say I think we need to demand, sir, if you could and your members, colleagues, that the RICO, Racketeer Influenced and Corrupt Organizations Act, which terrorism is a predicate for RICO, be used assiduously against the major terrorist organizations to go after their members, their money, and their facilities, knowing that we can use long-arm statutes like we did against this Banque Libano-Francaise to go after their money and correspondent bank accounts here, even if we can't get to it in Lebanon or Iran or somewhere in the Middle East.

So RICO is an absolutely central feature. It doesn't need to be legislated, but you could encourage its use. It has never been used in a large way, other than against the FARC, and that was quite successful.

Mr. DONOVAN. And as Dr. Levitt had said earlier, if we designate Hezbollah as a criminal enterprise, RICO then would be available to us.

Mr. LEVITT. RICO is available anyway. That would provide other benefits, but we could do RICO yesterday.

Mr. DONOVAN. Thank you.

Mr. Chairman, I yield back the remainder of my time.

Chairman ROYCE. Mr. Garrett?

Mr. GARRETT. Thank you, Mr. Chairman.

With the risk of—let me see how gentle I can be. I think we have missed the target here. As we discuss in this very meaningful and worthwhile hearing attacking Hezbollah's financial network tangentially, certainly we have discussed Iran, but I have a rather convoluted line chart here that I have done that shows Iran giving what is estimated to be, depending upon your source: Open source, $60 million to $200 million a year to Hezbollah; the IRGC controlling the entire black economy in Iran and big, large portions of the above-ground economy in Iran; and, just in the black economy side, controlling revenue between $25 billion and $50 billion a year and them supporting Iran. We have drug ops in Lebanon supporting Hezbollah, but the drug ops in Lebanon really took off after the Syrian civil war escalated, creating a vacuum. And when the LAF stopped patrolling the fields in the areas in the Beqaa Valley, we saw a skyrocketing production of drugs. So that was caused largely by Iran, who now has coopted the LAF to the point now where I recently read an article that said, "The distinction between Hezbollah and the Lebanese state is meaningless."

In fact, the Lebanese President is a Hezbollah ally, and the Lebanese were the only nation not to sign the resolution condemning the attacks on the Saudi consulate and Embassy in Iran, and so what we see here is we are talking about Hezbollah, but that is a branch on a tree. The tree should be called Iran. The roots of the tree should be called the IRGC. And if you want to solve the long-term problem, we need to take on the IRGC.

One of these gentlemen—and I apologize because I was copiously taking notes, so I don't know which of you it was—said we need to hold up to the agreement of the JCPOA, which I not jokingly referred to as the JCPOS—you can figure that one out—which means enforcing ballistic missile sanctions and, I quote: "Hold up to the agreements of the JCPOA, which means enforcing ballistic missile sanctions."

I wish—and I don't know how to do this because I am new here—that I could have read into the record an article from, of all places, NPR, which points out that the JCPOA is so tragically flawed that the lawyers that wrote it should be disbarred. Let me read to you from the U.N. Security Council Resolution 1929, which requires "Iran shall not undertake any activity related to ballistic missiles."

Fast forward to the JCPOA—if anybody knows this nod along with me—which reads: "Iran is called upon not to undertake any activity regarding ballistic missiles."

I am not that good a lawyer, but I know the difference between "shall not" and "called upon not to." And so we either intentionally sent really bad lawyers to negotiate a deal that puts Iran on a glidepath, not only to destroy sanctity and peace and stability in the region; we either intentionally did that or we hired the worst possible negotiators, who don't know the difference between "may" and "shall," which you learn as a first-year law student.

No enmity intended toward anyone in the room and particularly not the lady and gentlemen on the committee—I had to look, Dr. Karlin, to make sure—but would you not agree that the root of the problem with Hezbollah is Iran and that the root of the problem in Iran is the IRGC and that the root of the IRGC is Quds, if I want to walk this dog farther down the trail?

I mean, if we really want to attack the source of this, do we not look to the IRGC in returning peace and stability and functionality to Iran, whose people want it but whose people can't have it when the Quds Forces are willing to shoot student protestors in the head, right, with impunity, and the United States does nothing.

I apologize. I pride myself not on doing soliloquies and diatribes in these things, but I am frustrated because I think we are mistargeting. Would any one of you gentlemen or lady, is the root of the Hezbollah problem not Iran?

Mr. ASHER. Absolutely.

Mr. GARRETT. And is the root of the Iran problem——

Mr. ASHER. The IRGC, of course. And I worked to build a plan at CENTCOM where we went after the Iranians on various levels for various things that they did, including the IRGC, of which, unfortunately, much was abandoned as we got closer to the JCPOA. Whether you advocate a regime change or not, we don't accept the regime and its activities, and there is no way to divorce the IRGC from the Iranian economy and from the Lebanese state, in effect.

Mr. GARRETT. I am a big fan of peace and stability, and I advocate loud and vociferously on behalf of regime change. I don't think it needs to be done at the point of a gun, but I do think that we created circumstances in the JCPOA, and we have not pursued our allies, particularly in Europe, who do business with the IRGC, and we can do this with open sources documented to make them pick who they want to do business with.

Yes, sir?

Mr. LEVITT. Let me just put some meat on this bone, for example. The Financial Action Task Force gave Iran a year, a year that ends this month, to improve its behaviors on money laundering terror finance. Among the many things it is supposed to do are some very technical things and some very broad things. One of the things Iran has said it will not do is delete the cutout that it has for anything it describes as a resistance organization, i.e., Hezbollah. And it doesn't appear they are going to change that. That is this month, and we need to make sure that the administration makes its position very, very clear this is unacceptable for us because you will probably not get Iran off the FATF blacklist for special measures right now, but you will probably get them a little bit of an extension to see if they can do more.

Mr. GARRETT. Mr. Chairman, I am over time.

I wanted to say, in conclusion, we can have a regime change if we will strictly enforce sanctions. We have never been willing to do that. Hopefully this administration will change that. Thank you.

Chairman ROYCE. Thank you, Mr. Garrett.

We go now to, I think, Mr. Ted Yoho—oh, Mr. Gerry Connolly is here.

Mr. CONNOLLY. Thank you, Mr. Chairman.

Sorry, Ted.

Mr. YOHO. I yield.

Mr. CONNOLLY. I thank my friend from Florida.

Welcome, to the panel.

Dr. Karlin, are you familiar with the JCPOA?

Ms. KARLIN. Yes, sir, I am.

Mr. CONNOLLY. Was it an all-comprehensive agreement that covered all of Iranian behavior and our concerns?

Ms. KARLIN. I did not work on the JCPOA as an Obama administration official. My understanding is that it is primarily focused on the nuclear piece.

Mr. CONNOLLY. Correct. Can you think of a treaty governing an adversary that was all comprehensive in history?

Ms. KARLIN. Not off the top of my head.

Mr. CONNOLLY. Right. So, when President Kennedy, for example, negotiated the first Nuclear Test Ban Treaty to ban atmospheric testing of nuclear weapons with then Nikita Khrushchev and it was widely lauded as a peaceful measure, it didn't address other Soviet behaviors. Is that not correct?

Ms. KARLIN. Indeed. Usually, one——

Mr. CONNOLLY. Right. And when one looks at the JCPOA in terms of metrics, based on the fact that it was designed to curb and, in fact, reverse aspects of the nuclear development program in Iran, have those metrics been met, or is it widely agreed that Iran has, in fact, cheated and violated the terms of the agreement?

Ms. KARLIN. I think it is a complicated picture, and I am probably not the best person to address it.

Mr. CONNOLLY. I don't think it is complicated. By and large, all of the specific metrics with respect to the Iranian nuclear development program have, in fact, been met, which may be why we are trying to——

Mr. ASHER. Could I just make one interjection?

Mr. CONNOLLY. Excuse me, sir. No, please. And that may be why we want to divert attention sometimes in this hearing to other aspects of the Iranian behavior that indeed are to be decried and, to the best of our ability, sanctioned.

I take enormous exception to my colleague from Virginia asserting that maybe this administration will get serious about sanctions when the previous one did not. It was precisely because sanctions were working in the Group of 5, holding it together, that brought Iran to the table for the first time.

Ms. KARLIN. I couldn't agree more, sir.

Mr. CONNOLLY. And we don't get to rewrite history. You don't have to like it, but you don't get to rewrite it, and I think the record needed to be corrected.

So, maybe, Dr. Levitt or Dr. Karlin, but I am intrigued by Hezbollah's expanding role in the Syrian civil war, particularly, where they have been exposed. What is your sense, Dr. Levitt, of the cost? I mean, they have lost thousands of fighters. They have lost leadership. Has it weakened Hezbollah, or have they been able to use the exposure in Syria to their advantage in terms of strengthening the organization and its capabilities?

Mr. LEVITT. And the honest answer to that question is yes.

Mr. CONNOLLY. Yes, it has weakened them?

Mr. LEVITT. Yes, it has weakened them, and yes, it has strengthened them both. I thought Mara addressed this well in her remarks. Hezbollah had lost more people killed and more people wounded in this so far fairly brief conflict than in all the wars with Israel. It is costing Hezbollah a tremendous amount of money. The fighting in Syria is still getting the funds, but not everything in Lebanon that Hezbollah traditionally does—some of the other social welfare, political things are not. Again, showing the ties between military terrorism activities and political, social welfare activities, it is having an impact in terms of their supporters as well as some people's families are getting more money than other people, depending on how long you fought. The fact that they are now having to put up banners on the streets in Lebanon saying, "Well, if you don't really want to fight, you can make about a $1,000 donation and get out of it," it is like people are trying to get out of the forced conscription in Russia or Turkey back in the day.

Mr. CONNOLLY. Right.

Mr. ASHER. And so they are facing those types of problems. They have, however, had the benefit of the Islamic State rising to be such a threat that there has been a circling of the wagons in Lebanon—and elsewhere too, but we will focus on Lebanon—where the people say: I don't like Hezbollah, but Hezbollah is effectively defending me against the Islamic State, and so I don't have the luxury of still being angry at them for dragging my country, Lebanon, into the civil war.

Mr. CONNOLLY. Do you believe that the costs are hurting them back in Lebanon, either in terms of credibility, ability to recruit, or, for that matter, participate in whatever governance they participate in?

Mr. LEVITT. It is hurting them in terms of their ability to run their programs and their ability to recruit. There is dissension within the ranks among their supporters, but they are getting by just fine. And we need, therefore, right now to take the financial measures that will further undermine them.

All of your comments on the JCPOA I understand. Under the JCPOA, we were told these other things were going to continue. It is a fact that some of these were halted a little bit because some people felt they didn't want to shake the deal. I don't mean to make a statement about the deal there.

Now, we are where we are. Now is the opportunity to get back on the saddle here because we do have an opportunity to further exacerbate those financial tensions for Hezbollah.

Mr. CONNOLLY. Yes. And this is a test of a new administration, whether its close ties to Russia can be put to our advantage in terms of curbing the behavior of Hezbollah and the Iranian Revolutionary Guard in areas we care about: Syria and Iraq. And maybe it is time to now put that question to the new administration.

Thank you. My time is up.

Chairman ROYCE. Thank you.

We go now to Mr. Ted Yoho.

Mr. YOHO. Thank you, Mr. Chairman.

And I appreciate the panel being here.

I read an article about Hezbollah about a month ago and how it said that it has become a force of over 100,000 very well armed, very well trained, one of the top fighting forces in the world. And I am going to ask the panel—who wants to weigh in on this—was that possible before the JCPOA and the release of the money that Iran got, or did that benefit Hezbollah to become that strong of a force? Dr. Karlin?

Ms. KARLIN. Thank you for that question. That number is a little larger than I have heard, but the concept, I think, is absolutely spot on, that Hezbollah has grown. It has grown more capable quantitatively and qualitatively.

But we have seen it on this trajectory for a while now. Back in 2010 or so, my former boss Secretary Gates noted that Hezbollah had more missiles and rockets than most governments in the world. I would say the money has been useful, but it is the Syria conflict that has been determinative.

Mr. YOHO. Right. And that is where it was; it was in Syria, was the report I read. And they are not affiliated with a nation as far as a national government. They are kind of a proxy group, correct?

Ms. KARLIN. Hezbollah does serve in the Lebanese Government.

Mr. YOHO. Okay. And then, Mr. Levitt, I want to get clarification. Did you say that Iran should be redesignated as a state sponsor of terror?

Mr. LEVITT. Iran is designated a state sponsor of terror. There is no redesignation then.

Mr. YOHO. That is what I thought, and I misheard you then.

Mr. LEVITT. It was a response to a question about whether the context of redesignating Iranian entities that may have been taken off lists under the JCPOA and my argument that it would be in no way a violation of the JCPOA if they were relisted under still existing sanctions authorities like counterterrorism, which need to be very, very clear and show that evidence, that this is not simply just putting an entity back on the list for proliferation purposes.

Mr. YOHO. Okay.

And then, Dr. Asher, you had a comment you wanted to talk to Mr. Connolly about, and I will give you about 30 seconds if you want to add to it.

Mr. ASHER. So I respect Mr. Connolly's points about the JCPOA as a former negotiator in the Six Party Talks of North Korea and also working on North—Iran nuclear at one stage, but I am very concerned about outsourcing.

The thing we learned with North Korea in 2002 with the Al Kibar agreement was that countries can outsource. In 2002, there was an agreement between North Korea and Syria to build Al Kibar, the nuclear reactor for the nuclear weapons program with Syria. That broke ground in October 2003, according to unclassified information you can get on the internet. That is exactly when the NIE—the CIA—or the National Intelligence Council said the Iranians put their weapons program on hold. The idea that they could have outsourced it has always bothered me personally as an official at the time.

And then, in 2012, the Iranians and the North Koreans signed a science technology agreement that is almost exactly the same as what they signed with Syria between North Korea and Syria in 2002, and at the signing ceremony was Fereydoun Abbasi-Davani, the head of the Iranian nuclear weapons program. He just didn't show up very often to meetings. The question is, what is going on? And is it possible that Iran has outsourced? There is no provision in JCPOA over outsourcing, and it does worry me.

Mr. YOHO. All right.

And, Dr. Karlin, I want to come back to you. Is there continued production of heavy water in Iran, and does that come from nuclear activity?

Ms. KARLIN. I am not aware of that, sir.

Mr. YOHO. All right. I believe the answer is yes. Is the volume beyond what the JCPOA allows for, which, again, we have read the reports—they are producing more than they should be—and then is that production and value in violation of JCPOA? If they are doing that, would you say that was in violation?

Ms. KARLIN. If that were happening, that is beyond my expertise, sir.

Mr. YOHO. Can anybody else answer that?

All right. Mr. Maltz, I am going to go to you because the work you have done I find very interesting, and I don't know if it was you or Dr. Asher talking about the combination of the terrorist groups with the narcotrafficking. And do you see that increasing in the future?

Mr. MALTZ. Absolutely. I mean, everyone in government says that terrorists are increasingly turning to crime and criminal networks for funding because the U.S. Government and our allied forces have done such a great job at shutting down their funding streams. They need funds to operate, and one of the biggest things that I saw that is really disturbing is the corruption factor. You can't pay off a general in West Africa with a Visa and a Mastercard. You need a suitcase of cash.

Mr. YOHO. Right.

Mr. MALTZ. So the cash that is being generated from drug trafficking, the U.N. estimated, what, about $400 billion? So it is just common sense that they are going to get involved in drug trafficking and other illicit activity to be able to carry out their agenda. So, yes, I am very concerned, and it is evolving as far, as I am concerned.

Mr. YOHO. Do any of you believe that Hezbollah has been involved in the most recent Iranian kidnapping of the U.S. citizens or U.S. legal permanent residents? And if I don't have the time, Mr. Chairman, if they could submit that.

Chairman ROYCE. Is that a nod yes or a nod no? Pardon?

Mr. LEVITT. I have seen no evidence to that effect.

Mr. YOHO. Okay. Thank you. Chairman

ROYCE. All right. Thank you.

We go to Ann Wagner of Missouri. Ambassador.

Mrs. WAGNER. Thank you, Mr. Chairman, for hosting this hearing.

Hezbollah is obviously a constant violent threat to our allies and to us. The joint statement released by the U.S. and Saudi Arabia last month expressed the importance of supporting the Lebanese state in order to disarm Hezbollah. But I, along with many of my colleagues, are concerned that financial support to Lebanon may mean empowering Hezbollah.

Dr. Asher and Mr. Maltz, kind of as a follow-on to Congressman Yoho's questioning, it is well known that Syrian women and children are at risk of being trafficked in Lebanon. We also know that Hezbollah generates revenue from drug trafficking and, allegedly, human trafficking in the Americas.

Can you please discuss Hezbollah's involvement in human trafficking in Lebanon, Syria, and globally?

Mr. ASHER. I mean, I have one specific case I can't discuss, but I am aware of one of the top-tier targets; we call them super facilitators. We actually had a thing called the Iran-Hezbollah super facilitators initiative targeting key functional financiers for the Hezbollah-Iran network globally.

And I am aware of one very significant case of Syrian children being trafficked all the way into West Africa by an individual, and it was a very painful case for us because the U.S. Government was well aware of it, and we did nothing. And it still haunts me that these poor children—and they were like young girls and boys— were sent to a heinous country in West Africa probably to their death because the guy in charge seemed to like torturing children. So, you know, that is one case, and he was definitely a Hezbollah senior functional official also tied to the Iranians.

Mrs. WAGNER. Disturbing, but thank you, Dr. Asher.

Dr. Karlin, your testimony on Iran-Hezbollah relations was fascinating. Can Lebanon or other actors help fill a void with the Lebanese Shia who are dependent on Hezbollah, as your testimony laid out, in terms of political representation and economic opportunities? And could you also maybe flesh out for me the factors preventing these opportunities?

Ms. KARLIN. Thank you very much for that question. I am delighted that that was useful.

There are ways to fill this void, particularly if you look at strengthening Lebanon economically.

So what we have seen, because of the Syria conflict, is people who are joining Hezbollah because they don't have job opportunities and Hezbollah pays, obviously. So, to the extent you can look at microloans or other types of assistance so that, when you go into these areas where Hezbollah is strong, you actually see other entities there.

What I find most interesting on political representation, ma'am, is that you do hear some alternative voices to Hezbollah, but in particular, over the last few years, there were fewer and fewer people in Lebanon defending Hezbollah, and that quiet is meaningful and notable.

Mrs. WAGNER. Interesting. Well, Dr. Karlin, I will just stay with you for a moment. On Tuesday, we witnessed U.S.-led air strikes near al-Tanf and on the Iranian-backed militias in Syria. How interconnected are Hezbollah and these militias, and do you believe that economic sanctions on these militias could help stem Hezbollah's financing?

Ms. KARLIN. Thank you for that question. I, too, am really concerned about what is happening right now around al-Tanf. We see U.S. military getting more involved here, and it is very conceivable something could happen with these militias or with Hezbollah.

I think the Hezbollah-militia relationship is extremely tight. They are very much looking to one another. I defer to my colleagues regarding the financial piece, but my instinct is, if you can help weaken one, that is largely beneficial.

Mrs. WAGNER. Anyone else?

Mr. LEVITT. I will just add on two points, both of which are in my written testimony. One is, absolutely, we need to be targeting not just Hezbollah but the other Shia militias with which it is partnering very, very closely and, to get to some of the earlier questions, both of them together with Iranian soldiers and operatives on the ground in Syria. Al-Tanf is something we need to look at very, very closely. In the wake of that strike that you mentioned, Hezbollah issued a kind of veiled warning to the U.S. not to cross its—Hezbollah's—red lines in the area.

Mrs. WAGNER. Uh-huh.

Mr. LEVITT. And the other thing regarding Dr. Asher's comment on the super facilitators, I mentioned briefly in my oral remarks the need to target these key networks, and my written testimony gets into detail that we should be targeting, among those, the super facilitators, some of whom, I think including the one that Dr. Asher was referring to, are really—they are Hezbollah people. Others are not. Others, they are not Hezbollah operatives. They are criminals. They are super facilitators who will help Hezbollah today and some other criminal enterprise tomorrow, but they play these mission critical roles, whether it is money laundering or accessing banks. And we should be targeting them as well, even if they are not card-carrying Hezbollah members, because they are providing mission critical, particularly logistic and financial, support to Hezbollah.

Mrs. WAGNER. I thank you all.

And I thank you, Mr. Chairman. I believe I am out of time, and I will yield back.

Chairman ROYCE. We are out of time, but thank you very much, Ambassador Wagner.

We appreciate the time, the service, and the expertise of our witnesses here this morning. And as we have heard, there is much work to be done to rebuild our law enforcement capabilities to tackle Hezbollah, and we look forward to working with our witnesses as we press the administration to do just that.

Thank you very much. We stand adjourned.

[Whereupon, at 11:54 a.m., the committee was adjourned.]

APPENDIX

MATERIAL SUBMITTED FOR THE RECORD

FULL COMMITTEE HEARING NOTICE
COMMITTEE ON FOREIGN AFFAIRS
U.S. HOUSE OF REPRESENTATIVES
WASHINGTON, DC 20515-6128

Edward R. Royce (R-CA), Chairman

June 8, 2017

TO: MEMBERS OF THE COMMITTEE ON FOREIGN AFFAIRS

You are respectfully requested to attend an OPEN hearing of the Committee on Foreign Affairs, to be held in Room 2172 of the Rayburn House Office Building (and available live on the Committee website at http://www.ForeignAffairs.house.gov):

DATE: Thursday, June 8, 2017

TIME: 10:00 a.m.

SUBJECT: Attacking Hezbollah's Financial Network: Policy Options

WITNESSES: Matthew Levitt, Ph.D.
Director and Fromer-Wexler Fellow
Stein Program on Counterterrorism and Intelligence
The Washington Institute for Near East Policy

David Asher, Ph.D.
Member
Board of Directors
Center on Sanctions and Illicit Finance
Foundation for Defense of Democracies

Mr. Derek Maltz
Executive Director
Governmental Relations
Pen-Link, Ltd.

Mara Karlin, Ph.D.
Associate Professor of Practice and Associate Director of Strategic Studies
School for Advanced International Studies
Johns Hopkins University

By Direction of the Chairman

COMMITTEE ON FOREIGN AFFAIRS
MINUTES OF FULL COMMITTEE HEARING

Day __*Thursday*__ Date ___*6/8/2017*___ Room ___*2172*___

Starting Time ___*10:08*___ Ending Time ___*11:55*___

Recesses | *0* | (___ to ___) (___ to ___) (___ to ___) (___ to ___) (___ to ___) (___ to ___)

Presiding Member(s)
Chairman Edward R. Royce

Check all of the following that apply:

Open Session ☑
Executive (closed) Session ☐
Televised ☑

Electronically Recorded (taped) ☑
Stenographic Record ☑

TITLE OF HEARING:

Attacking Hezbollah's Financial Network: Policy Options

COMMITTEE MEMBERS PRESENT:

See attached.

NON-COMMITTEE MEMBERS PRESENT:

none

HEARING WITNESSES: Same as meeting notice attached? Yes ☑ No ☐
(If "no", please list below and include title, agency, department, or organization.)

STATEMENTS FOR THE RECORD: *(List any statements submitted for the record.)*

IFR - Rep. Thomas Garrett
IFR - Rep. Ted Deutch
SFR - Rep. Gerald Connolly
QFR - Rep. Chris Smith
QFR - Rep. Michael McCaul

TIME SCHEDULED TO RECONVENE _________
or
TIME ADJOURNED *11:55*

Full Committee Hearing Coordinator

HOUSE COMMITTEE ON FOREIGN AFFAIRS
FULL COMMITTEE HEARING

PRESENT	MEMBER	PRESENT	MEMBER
X	Edward R. Royce, CA		Eliot L. Engel, NY
	Christopher H. Smith, NJ		Brad Sherman, CA
X	Ileana Ros-Lehtinen, FL		Gregory W. Meeks, NY
X	Dana Rohrabacher, CA		Albio Sires, NJ
	Steve Chabot, OH	X	Gerald E. Connolly, VA
X	Joe Wilson, SC	X	Theodore E. Deutch, FL
	Michael T. McCaul, TX		Karen Bass, CA
X	Ted Poe, TX	X	William Keating, MA
	Darrell Issa, CA	X	David Cicilline, RI
	Tom Marino, PA		Ami Bera, CA
X	Jeff Duncan, SC		Lois Frankel, FL
	Mo Brooks, AL	X	Tulsi Gabbard, HI
X	Paul Cook, CA	X	Joaquin Castro, TX
X	Scott Perry, PA		Robin Kelly, IL
X	Ron DeSantis, FL		Brendan Boyle, PA
X	Mark Meadows, NC		Dina Titus, NV
X	Ted Yoho, FL	X	Norma Torres, CA
	Adam Kinzinger, IL	X	Brad Schneider, IL
X	Lee Zeldin, NY		Tom Suozzi, NY
X	Dan Donovan, NY	X	Adriano Espaillat, NY
	James F. Sensenbrenner, Jr., WI	X	Ted Lieu, CA
X	Ann Wagner, MO		
	Brian J. Mast, FL		
X	Brian K. Fitzpatrick, PA		
	Francis Rooney, FL		
X	Thomas A. Garrett, Jr., VA		

MATERIAL SUBMITTED FOR THE RECORD BY THE HONORABLE THOMAS A. GARRETT, JR., A REPRESENTATIVE IN CONGRESS FROM THE COMMONWEALTH OF VIRGINIA

parallels

Did Iran's Ballistic Missile Test Violate A U.N. Resolution?

February 3, 2017 · 12:27 PM ET

PETER KENYON

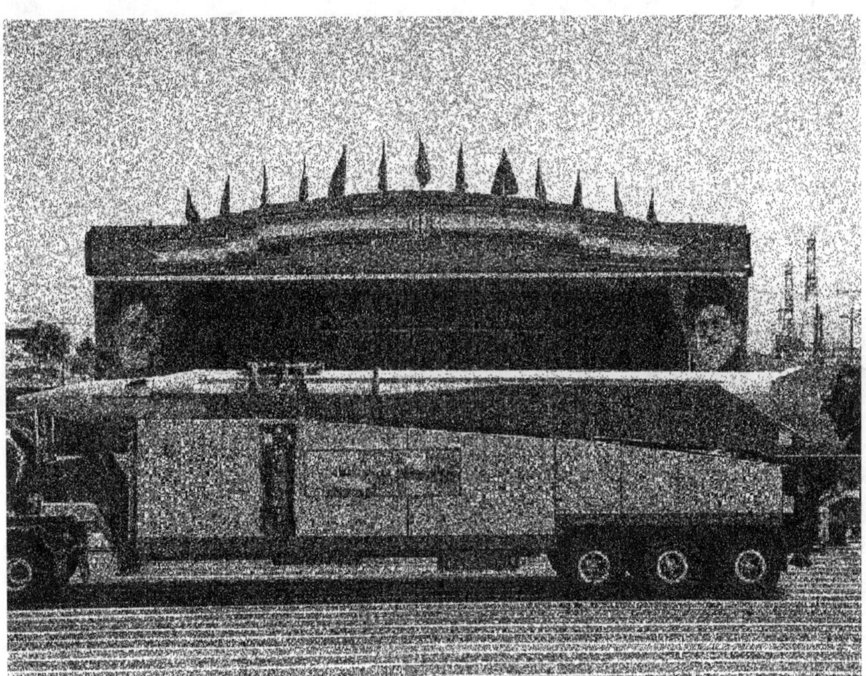

An Emad ballistic missile is displayed by the Revolutionary Guard during a September 2016 military parade in front of the shrine of Iran's revolutionary founder Ayatollah Khomeini, just outside Tehran. Iranian Foreign Minister Mohammad Javad Zarif has said Iran's missile program is not part of a 2015 landmark nuclear deal between his country and world powers.

Ebrahim Noroozi/AP

In the days leading up to today's announcement of additional U.S. sanctions on Iran, the U.S. and Iran have made claims and counter-claims as to whether Iran's ballistic missile test on Sunday violated a U.N. Security Council resolution and the 2015 nuclear deal between Iran and six world powers, including the U.S.

U.S. Treasury Department Announces New Sanctions On Iran

"Iran is playing with fire," President Trump tweeted Friday morning before the sanctions were announced. Trump's National Security Adviser, Lt. Gen. Mike Flynn, earlier said the missile test was "in defiance of" U.N. Security Council Resolution 2231 endorsing the Iran nuclear deal. White House Press Secretary Sean Spicer called the test an outright "violation."

Iran's foreign minister, Mohammad Javad Zarif, meanwhile tweeted that Iran is "unmoved" by U.S. threats and has the right to defend itself.

So did Iran violate the agreement or not?

Javad Zarif
@JZarif

Iran unmoved by threats as we derive security from our people. We'll never initiate war, but we can only rely on our own means of defense.
6:48 AM - 3 Feb 2017

4,024   9,739

Most nonproliferation experts would say Iran certainly defied the spirit of the U.N. resolution, but technically didn't violate it — because it contains no prohibition against such testing, as one of its predecessors, passed in 2010, specifically did.

Here's what the two resolutions say on the subject, with highlighting added:

U.N. Security Council Resolution 1929, from 2010, says the Security Council "decides that Iran **shall not undertake any activity** related to ballistic missiles capable of delivering nuclear weapons, including launches using ballistic missile technology, and that States shall take all necessary measures to prevent the transfer of technology or technical assistance to Iran related to such activities."

In Resolution 2231, passed in 2015, the Security Council endorsed the nuclear deal, known formally as the Joint Comprehensive Plan of Action or JCPOA. It terminated the provisions of the 2010 resolution and added language deep in one of the annexes saying: "Iran is **called upon not to undertake any activity** related to ballistic missiles designed to be capable of delivering nuclear weapons, including launches using such ballistic missile technology, until the date eight years after the JCPOA Adoption Day or until the date on which the IAEA submits a report confirming the Broader Conclusion, whichever is earlier."

As diplomatic terms of art, "shall not" — which appeared in the 2010 resolution — represents a clear and enforceable prohibition, whereas being "called upon" not to do something is more ambiguous.

Here's one way to look at it: When Iran tested ballistic missiles in the fall of 2015, while Resolution 1929 was still in effect, it was doubtless in violation of a Security Council stricture. But when it tested its missile on Sunday, under the new Resolution 2231, Iran was essentially ignoring the Security Council's advice — not violating a directive.

Conservative critics of the nuclear agreement argued strongly against the language change, calling it a dangerous watering-down of the international position on Iran's ballistic missile program.

Iran has long maintained that its missile tests don't violate Security Council resolutions because there are no nuclear warheads involved and Iran's conventional defenses are its own business. But both the 2010 and 2015 resolutions do warn against testing missiles that "could be capable" of carrying a nuclear warhead.

"For its part, Iran says it never agreed to missile restrictions in the JCPOA and claims its missile tests do not violate Security Council resolutions because they are not designed to carry nuclear warheads. This is absurd," former CIA analyst Fred Fleitz argued in The National Review last year. "Iran's missile program is widely believed to be a delivery system for nuclear warheads. If Iran were telling the truth, it would be the only nation in history without a nuclear-weapons program that nonetheless developed missiles with a range of 2,000 kilometers or more. Iran is not building long-range missiles to carry warheads full of dynamite or to fire monkeys into space."

In fact, the Obama administration had argued for keeping in place the stronger prohibitory language of Resolution 1929, but it lost that argument when its negotiating partners wouldn't back the Americans up.

"When Mr. Obama sought to include a prohibition on ballistic missiles in the Iran deal, or at least extend a previous Security Council resolution banning them, not just Russia and China but even our European allies in the nuclear negotiations refused," former Obama White House official Philip Gordon explained this week in the New York Times. "They argued that the ballistic missile ban was put in place in 2010 only to pressure Iran to reach a nuclear deal, and they refused to extend it once that deal had been concluded."

The question remains, what next? In a short briefing paper on Iran's missile testing, analysts at the Iran Project, a non-governmental group including former diplomats say the challenge for President Trump is to "constrain Iran's missile testing while maintaining the U.S. and Iranian commitment to the JCPOA, the most assured way to prevent Iran from acquiring a nuclear weapon."

The Security Council scheduled "urgent consultations" on Iran's missile test earlier this week.

Gordon, the former White House official, noted that Iranian presidential elections this spring will likely prompt hardliners to stake out a position of defiance in the missile dispute. The stage would seem to be set for tough rhetoric to escalate, he wrote, including the possibility of terrorist attacks on Americans in the Mideast.

missile test   united nations   iran

Get The Stories That Grabbed Us This Week

Delivered to your inbox every Sunday, these are the NPR stories that keep us scrolling.

What's your email?

• • • • • • •• •

By subscribing, you agree to NPR's terms of use and privacy policy.

More Stories From NPR

Material submitted for the record by the Honorable Theodore E. Deutch, a Representative in Congress from the State of Florida

June 7, 2017

The Honorable Edward R. Royce
Chair
House Foreign Affairs Committee
U.S. House of Representatives
Washington, D.C. 20515

The Honorable Eliot L. Engel
Ranking Member
House Foreign Affairs Committee
U.S. House of Representatives
Washington, D.C. 20515

Dear Chairman Royce and Ranking Member Engel,

In advance of tomorrow's full Committee hearings entitled "Attacking Hezbollah's Financial Network: Policy Options," we write to provide the views of the Anti-Defamation League (ADL) and ask that this statement be included as part of the official hearings record.

The Anti-Defamation League

Founded in 1913, the Anti-Defamation League (ADL) is the nation's foremost non-governmental authority on domestic terrorism and extremism, and organized hate groups and hate crimes. Researchers in our National Office in New York and investigators in the field monitor, analyze, and expose the full range of domestic extremist groups and international terrorist organizations. The League maintains comprehensive, frequently-updated informational resources for law enforcement personnel engaged in combating extremism and criminal activity. ADL is a strong advocate of a secure State of Israel at peace with its neighbors, and as such works to expose those who threaten and seek to destabilize the Jewish state.

We very much appreciate the Committee holding this hearing examining the possibility of additional tools to target Hezbollah's financial resources. The Committee has been a vital bulwark against terrorism and, specifically, against Hezbollah, including support for the Hezbollah International Financing Prevention Act of 2015.

Targeting Hezbollah's Financial Networks

ADL would support additional legislation designed to limit the influence, capability, and reach of Hezbollah, the Lebanese-based terror organization that is responsible for the loss of many American lives. Hezbollah continues to pose a threat to a key United States ally, Israel, and is one of the main actors in Syria responsible for perpetrating atrocities against the Syrian people.

While examining further actions against Hezbollah, we urge the Committee to consider the following initiatives:

- Applying secondary sanctions to financial entities connected to Hezbollah and/or its associates.

- Identifying, designating, and sanctioning more individuals belonging to the organization's leadership cadre.

- Highlighting Iran's role in financing Hezbollah and assessing ways to stem the cash and arms flow from Tehran.

- Investigating and exposing intelligence and logistical support networks in the Latin American region. Despite the public exposure of Iranian and Hezbollah operatives in the deadly 1994 bombing of the AMIA Jewish community center in Buenos Aires, Argentina, Hezbollah continues to enjoy financial benefit through relations with regional-based transnational criminal organizations.

We appreciate the opportunity to provide our views to the Committee on this issue of high priority to our organization. Please do not hesitate to contact us if we can provide additional information or if we can be of assistance in any way as the Committee considers further action against this dangerous, potent threat to US interests in the Middle East.

Sincerely,

Kenneth Jacobson
Deputy National Director
Anti-Defamation League

Statement for the Record
Submitted by Mr. Connolly of Virginia

Hezbollah is a multifaceted terrorist organization that has been deeply embedded in Lebanese society for decades. Iran's Islamic Revolutionary Guard Corps is directly responsible for the group's creation and continues to be its primary source of arms and funding. Hezbollah has been a significant force in Lebanese politics since the early 1990s, and currently holds twelve seats in Parliament and two cabinet posts. Hezbollah supported the candidacy of Lebanese President Michel Aoun, who was elected on October 31, 2016. President Aoun's Free Patriotic Movement declared an alliance with Hezbollah in 2006 and Aoun has come under fire for comments supporting Hezbollah's armament during his short presidency. Since its founding, Hezbollah has engaged in terrorism and other destabilizing activities that threaten the security interests of the United States and our allies, especially Israel.

I remember vividly the bombings of the U.S. Embassy and Marine barracks in Beirut in 1983. The attack on our embassy killed 63 people and more than 240 American military personnel perished in the suicide bombing at the barracks just a few months later. The attack on the barracks especially was a shock to the nation's security psyche, and it ushered in a new, grim era of international terrorist attacks.

Israel and Hezbollah have fought several wars, including one in 2006 in which Hezbollah killed 160 Israelis and launched 4,000 missiles into Israel. To this day, the group maintains a missile arsenal that can strike any corner of Israel. To counter these missile-borne threats and other security challenges, last year the Obama Administration made the largest single pledge of military assistance in U.S. history. Under the new Memorandum of Understanding (MOU) with Israel, the United States will provide $33 billion in Foreign Military Financing and $5 billion in missile defense assistance over the next ten years, a significant increase over the previous MOU. The U.S. commitment to Israel's security rests, in part, on a determined effort to support Israel's ability to defend itself against attacks from Hezbollah.

Hezbollah's violence extends beyond Lebanon and Israel. Since at least 2013, Hezbollah has conducted military operations in Syria where it reportedly maintains between 4,000 and 8,000 fighters on behalf of President Bashar al-Assad. Last year, Hezbollah field commanders stated that Russia is supplying them with long-range tactical missiles, laser-guided rockets, and anti-tank weapons in exchange for intelligence and assistance in target selection. Hezbollah personnel have played a significant role in efforts to control land transportation routes between Iran and Lebanon, in addition to key battles such as the recapture of Aleppo from opposition control. This has not come without a cost. The group has reportedly suffered more than a thousand casualties, including several senior leaders, and invited the enmity of many Arab countries that oppose the Assad regime.

Last year, the member countries of the Arab League and Gulf Cooperation Council joined the United States, Canada, the Netherlands, and Israel in designating Hezbollah in its entirety as a terrorist organization. However, the European Union continues to distinguish between the "military" and "political" wings of Hezbollah and has only added the military wing to its terrorist list. More must be done to drive an international consensus regarding Hezbollah if we hope to counter the destabilizing role it plays in the region. In an effort to do just that, I have cosponsored H. Res. 359, introduced by my colleague Rep. Ted Deutch, which would urge the European Union to designate Hezbollah in its entirety as a terrorist organization and increase pressure on the group.

In December 2015, Congress passed and the President enacted into law legislation authored by Chairman Royce and Ranking Member Engel – the Hezbollah International Financing Prevention Act of 2015 (PL 114-102). The authorities included in the legislation have enhanced the ability of the Treasury Department to target entities that provide the group with financial support as well as entities that conduct transactions with foreign financial institutions that work with Hezbollah.

As a result of these and other international sanctions, Hezbollah is undergoing a financial crisis that has prompted the party to seek additional support through fundraising campaigns to equip its fighters. In addition to the funding it receives from Iran, Hezbollah has developed a global criminal network from the Balkans, to Southwest Asia, to South America, and Africa. Hezbollah's criminal enterprises include drug trafficking, procuring false passports, money laundering, and corporate front organizations. I look forward to hearing from our witnesses regarding the ways in which Congress can disrupt Hezbollah's sprawling financial network while ensuring that we do not destabilize Lebanon.

Questions for the Record
Rep. Chris Smith
HFAC Full Committee Hearing
"Attacking Hezbollah's Financial Network: Policy Options"
June 8, 2017

1. Do Hezbollah and other Shia terrorist groups ascribe to any general doctrinal guidelines concerning the treatment of hostages and their release for ransom? How does this approach compare and contrast with that of Sunni jihadist groups, such as ISIS, Jabhat Fatah al-Sham, and al-Qa'eda? Does Hezbollah have a practice of beheading or otherwise executing prisoners, even in cases in which ransom is paid? Are there doctrinal or tactical disagreements among Shia terrorist groups and the IRGC concerning the taking of hostages, their treatment, and release for ransom?

   What does the Lebanese hostage crisis of 1982-1992, including the death of CIA Station Chief William Francis Buckley, say about the organization's approach and how it may or may not have evolved over time?

Asher: Hezbollah has become a much more advanced and sophisticated criminal terrorist organization. Wanton killing ala Chief of Station Buckley is old school for them. Today they are a Warfighting group that is the most advanced form of mafia mixed with military. Evolution for them is devolution for us, hence why we can't understand what they do today as "beyond terrorism."

2. Based on your understanding of how Hezbollah collects and disburses money, what additional measures do you recommend that the United States take to staunch the growth of Shia terrorist groups in Bahrain? Are there any measures we can take to get ahead of the curve of the development of these groups into even more threatening organizations?

Asher: The US needs to realize that Hezbollah is impregnated into every Lebanese financial institution as well into Bahrain and Qatar. The Linchpin are leftover elements of the PLO. They are all designated terrorist groups and networks but are not easy to pin down for the simple minded who don't believe there is such a thing as Sunni and Shia crossover on revolution....

Questions for the Record
Rep. Michael McCaul
HFAC Full Committee Hearing
"Attacking Hezbollah's Financial Network: Policy Options"
June 8, 2017

<u>Iran and Hezbollah</u>

The IRGC is responsible for the creation of Hezbollah and has been the main entity funding, training, and equipping this terror organization. As you know, on December 18, 2015, the President signed into law the Hizbollah International Financing Prevention Act of 2015. This law targets parties that facilitate financial transactions for Hezbollah's benefit.

1. How effective has this law been in disrupting Hezbollah's financial network and what more can the U.S. Government do to crack down on IRGC support to Hezbollah?

Levitt: Hundreds of Hezbollah-linked bank accounts have been closed since Congress passed HIPFA in 2015. However, Hezbollah continues to bypass the legislation by storing funds outside of Lebanon, in Dubai and Iraq, for example. Evidently, Hezbollah is able to collect sufficient funds to maintain a significant militia in Lebanon and Syria, send smaller operative groups to Iraq and Yemen, and operate an international terrorist network.

The United States must lead an international effort to target the group's illicit financial conduct both at home in Lebanon and around the world. These efforts are not intended to undermine the Lebanese economy, rather, to shield it from exposure to the criminal and money laundering enterprises that Hezbollah continues to exploit.

In order to counter IRGC support to Hezbollah, the U.S. may, without undermining the JCPOA, sanction state sponsors of terror, such as the IRGC. In February 2017, Treasury designated Hasan Dehghan Ebrahimi, an IRGC affiliate in Beirut. This was a good start and the US should continue to sanction individuals and organizations affiliated with Iranian sponsors of state terror.

Asher: The IRGC operates via Hezbollah's Islamic Jihad organization. It is an appendage of Tehran more than Beirut and needs to be treated as such. Efforts to treat them separately are bound to fail and up to now we have failed to have an impact, simply put....Our legal efforts have been grossly ineffective at hitting them organizationally for decades. Our counter terrorist whackamole has been tactically effective but not strategic.

<u>Impact of Gulf Crisis on Hezbollah</u>

In March, the Gulf Cooperation Council (GCC) and the Arab League classified Hezbollah, a Lebanese Islamist political and military organization, as a terrorist group. The GCC – comprised of Saudi Arabia, Qatar, the United Arab Emirates, Oman, Bahrain, and Kuwait – made the decision on March 2, accusing Hezbollah of "incitement in Syria, Yemen, and in Iraq." This was the first instance of a regional grouping designating Hezbollah in its entirety as a terrorist organization.

2. How does the most recent rift in relations between members of the GCC and the Qatari Government impact cooperation on this front?

Levitt: The ongoing tension between Qatar and other GCC states is unlikely to impact the GCC designation of Hezbollah as such, but it may distract GCC focus from the issue of Hezbollah and the Iran Threat Network. While Hezbollah has a history of carrying out attacks in countries such as Kuwait and Saudi Arabia, Hezbollah has not had a large presence in Qatar. Additionally, Qatar played a minimal role in the March 2016 decision to designate Hezbollah as a terrorist organization. Therefore, in contrast to other GCC members, Qatar has less at stake in the 2016 designation and it is unlikely that the current Gulf rift will affect the GCC designation.

Asher: Iran has set Hezbollah on a course of subversion and destruction with Qatar. Qatar needs to abandon a model of doing business with the highest bidder and most coercive player in the mob and approach business on the basis of strategic alliances. If they think Iran and Hezbollah are true allies then we have a real problem on our hands...

3. How do you expect Hezbollah may attempt to capitalize on the instability between GCC countries and the rest of the Arab world?

Levitt: It is possible for Hezbollah to take advantage of the ongoing instability and rift in the Gulf region right now. Since June, Saudi Arabia and the rest of the GCC block have been preoccupied with the ongoing blockade against Qatar. They are likely distracted from dealing with threats from Hezbollah.

This could be an issue for the GCC, considering that the Syrian war has shifted Hezbollah's focus from battling Israel to engaging in new, regional, pan-Shi`a focused conflicts. Hezbollah has also become more aggressive in the Gulf as a result of the sustained geopolitical and sectarian tensions between Saudi Arabia and Iran.

With the notable exception of Syria, Hezbollah's regional reorientation is most obvious in its increased presence in the Gulf. In 2013, a Hezbollah sleeper cell was busted in the United Arab Emirates. In 2015, Hezbollah members were arrested in Bahrain, and that same year, Kuwaiti authorities raided a terrorist cell of 26 Shi`a Kuwaitis with links to Iran and Hezbollah. In light of these and other threats, as well as the fact that the Gulf block is distracted with the GCC rift, Hezbollah could attempt to take advantage of the ongoing instability in the Gulf.

Asher: Iran is in the driver's seat. Hezbollah is a willing pawn. Expect more instability since this is what Tehran wants. They will fight to the last Lebanese. Witness Syria.....

TCO-Terrorism Nexus

In recent years, we have seen terrorist organizations and transnational criminal organizations interact in similar and significant ways. This includes shared tactics such as money laundering, undetected cross-border movements, illegal weapons acquisition, and the exploitation of corrupt government officials.

In the case of terrorism, I think their increased resiliency is due in part to their combination of state support as well as their expansion into profitable illicit activities, similar to those of a transnational criminal organization.

Mr. Asher – in your opening statement you laid out a somewhat specific blueprint on how in 2008, the U.S. government integrated its efforts to spearhead the implementation of a strategy to pursue Hezbollah's web of illicit activities and finances.

4. How do you all distinguish between the efforts we employ to attack a terror organization like Hezbollah's financial network from the efforts deployed to combat transnational criminal organizations?

Levitt: Hezbollah is not designated by most of the world as a terrorist organization. Therefore, demonstrating that Hezbollah is engaging in criminal activities, in addition to terrorism, may be a powerful means of building international cooperation to target Hezbollah. Furthermore, designating Hezbollah as a transnational criminal organization (TCO) enables the U.S. and others to target Hezbollah without having to prove that they were buying weapons or engaging in explicitly terrorist related activities. Classifying Hezbollah as a TCO recognizes the reality that Hezbollah's activities extend beyond the realm of terrorism.

The State Department, Department of Defense, and the Department of Justice have worked to address the criminal aspects of terrorist organizations, as seen in the creation of the Counterterrorism Partnership Fund (CTPF) in 2014. One strength of the CTFP was how it raised awareness about Iran's and Hezbollah's broad ranges of terrorist and criminal activities around the world and increased law enforcement cooperation and coordination among a wide range of countries to disrupt these activities. This is one example of how to address CT and criminal group issues in tandem.

Lastly, designating Hezbollah as a TCO affects their domestic and international reputation. Hezbollah is very sensitive to being portrayed at home in Lebanon as well as in the international area as illegitimate or criminal, and is concerned with Lebanon's and other countries' willingness to take action against them. This is why it is critical to name and shame Hezbollah and its operatives for the criminal enterprise they have become.

Asher: There should be no fundamental difference. The statues that applied to Al Capone, apply to Hezbollah, except that we have extraordinary and exigent statues like 959, 960, and 981(k) that supersede and traverse. Our government is deficient in seeking results versus sound bites.....

5. What authorities do agencies currently have to go after terrorist organizations that don't exist when we are pursuing transnational criminal organizations?

Levitt: The authorities that intelligence agencies currently have to go after terrorist organization would complement the authorities they have to pursue transnational criminal organizations. A key benefit would be to enable agencies to target those criminal entities that serve as facilitators for terrorist groups. Furthermore, counterterrorism efforts are by no means undermined by complimenting them with efforts tailored to counter criminal activities. When such efforts are properly coordinated, measures to counter criminal activities of a criminal organization should in no way impede ongoing intelligence collection or operations.

Asher: In a word, RICO. RICO is our most powerful and productive tool against terrorists but we don't seem to have to resolve to apply it.